Surfacing –

Sequel to 'Surviving Schizophrenia'

by
Louise Gillett

Published by Twynham Press
Paperback 1st edition

ISBN 978-095669377-8

i

Twynham Press

Copyright © Louise Gillett 2015

This book is dedicated to my family.

I love you all.

CONTENTS

PART ONE   Page

1. Surfacing   1

2. The Day Hospital   6

3. Schizophrenia   12

4. Dropping another Bombshell   15

5. Coco   20

6. Bunions (oh, the glamour!)   24

7. The Alexander Technique   34

8. The Church Connection
        36

9. Grammar School   38

10. Cognitive Behavioural Therapy   41

11. Ghost-Writing   46

12. The Schizophrenia Commission   49

13. Raymond Briggs   53

14. Dealing with Criticism   58

15. A New School Year   61

16. The Schizophrenia Commission Report   62

17. Growing Up   64

18. Newcastle University   68

19. Rethink Members Day 2012, Nottingham   73

20. A Meeting with the Department for
    Work and Pensions   78

21. National Psychosis Summit, April 2014   80

22. The McPin Foundation   83

23. Book Reviews   85

24. The Diagnosis   88

25. Majorca   92

26. A Day at Roedean   95

27. Everyone Judges a Book by its Cover   98

28. Summer 2014   100

29. The End (I hope)   101

PART TWO

ON LIVING   103

WHAT WOULD HAVE HELPED?

1. WRITING   107

2. READING   113

3. SELF CARE   117

4. GETTING BUSY   120

5. REJECTING THE DIAGNOSIS   124

6. LOOKING OUTSIDE THE MENTAL
   HEALTH SYSTEM   134

7. GETTING MY MIND ON SIDE   143

8. NOT CARING   146

9. FOSTERING INDEPENDENCE   148

10. A PET   150

AND FINALLY   151

PART ONE

CHAPTER ONE
Surfacing

It is the morning rush hour in Bournemouth, and I am nearing my destination. I left home half-an-hour ago and, although I did not have far to travel, I am still slowly navigating my dark-blue Vauxhall Zafira through the heavy traffic. I have to be extra careful, because there is precious cargo aboard – my two little girls are sitting side-by-side in the seats behind me. Although, of course, my daughters are not so small these days – Anna is now eleven and Amy is nine years old.

My girls are beautiful. Anna has long, wavy, brown hair and a steady and composed look. She is an older version of the wide-eyed baby girl who another mother had once told me appeared so 'grounded'. She is my star, my flagship and the reason why I pressed on to have three more children with my beloved, and wearily acquiescent, husband. Anna is a top student. She is also a darling and a sweetheart and I adore her.

Amy is a giggling, gorgeous bundle of fun. She has the Dutch colouring of her father's side of the family - bright blue eyes and thick, strong, extra-long white-blonde hair. She is smart too, like her sister. Amy is the centre of attention wherever she goes, and she revels in it. I love her and I constantly marvel at her.

My mind is on my daughters as I drive. I am heading towards a location that I have tried to put to the back of my mind for many years. A place they don't even know exists and that, even if they did, they would never in a million years associate with their mother. A mental hospital.

A lot of things are about to change in my daughters' understanding of the world.

I decided on this trip less than an hour ago. It is the start of the school summer holidays. Anna and Amy's two younger brothers are at their grandparents' house, where they have spent the night. Scott and Luke like to visit Oma and Opa, as they term Paul's parents. The welcome mat is always rolled out for them there.

Paul's Mum and Dad live in a ground floor flat, immaculate in a manner that perhaps only the homes of retired couples can be. They have a spare bedroom there, with twin beds always made up ready for the grandchildren. There is a tried and tested routine for sleepovers. The boys, I know, will have eaten sausage and chips for dinner last night, and pancakes with strawberries this morning. I don't like any of my children being away from home overnight, even with their grandparents, but I know that occasionally it is good for them, and for me. And for the oldies too, of course.

The main benefit of a sleepover for the boys, as far as I am concerned, is that it gives Paul and I the opportunity to spend some time with the girls, undistracted by their noisy younger brothers. We'd had a peaceful evening together and now, the next day, I am not due to pick the boys up until lunchtime. It is a weekday, so Paul is at work. Usually, on the rare occasions when it is just the three of us, I take the girls swimming or to the beach – somewhere fun and exciting. I am an attentive mother, and normally a trip to a mental hospital would not be my idea of a fun excursion for my daughters.

However, I have been distracted in recent weeks. I recently published a book about my life, and it contains some shocking information. I realise now that I need to tell my daughters about this book and its contents, before anybody else reads it and tells them for me. The problem is that I don't know where to start.

So I slowly drive along, paying meticulous attention to the road and the traffic because I have two of the most important people in the world on board this vehicle with me. Eventually, I begin to talk.

'Do you want to know where we are going, girls?'

Of course they do.

'Well, we're going to a place where Mummy spent a lot of time, before either of you was born. It's a hospital. Once, a long time ago, I was very ill, in my...in my brain. Or my mind'.

'What sort of ill?' Anna asks.

'I went mad'.

Amy laughs and Anna joins in, but their voices sound hollow, uncertain.

'It's not a joke,' I tell them, but I laugh too because I understand that they are nervous and I don't want them to feel rebuked. 'I wasn't dangerous,' I add hurriedly. 'I never hurt anybody. But I was very ill. And I was taken to hospital, where I had to stay. Not the place we are going to visit now. This one is a day hospital. I didn't have to go there, but I did, every day for years'.

'Why?' That's Amy talking now. At least, I tell myself, I know that they are both listening. Because I really don't want to have to start repeating myself. It is hard enough having to say this once.

'Well, I suppose because I didn't know what else to do. The doctors and nurses all told me I was never going to get better and that I would need to take medication – pills – for the rest of my life. And I believed them. So I came along every day, to learn about the illness, and also to watch television and talk to the other patients and the nurses. They fed us well'. It sounds lame, even to me. Why on earth had I willingly attended a mental hospital every day for years, I wonder? Because I was helpless and hopeless, I silently answer myself.

'But you're okay now, Mummy,' Anna says. I know that she just wants me to say that yes, I am okay, and that she hopes that I will then shelve this expedition, drop the subject, and take the pair of them off to buy some ice-cream instead. I take a deep breath and plough on.

'I am okay now, darling. I'm completely fine. I'm more than fine, now, because I have you four children and Daddy, and really I have never been happier in my whole life. But I – well, I wrote a book about what happened to me. Because I wanted to explain to other people that anybody can go mad, and that anybody can get better too. So that people won't feel so bad if it happens to them or to someone they love. Because the worst thing for me about being mentally ill – about being

4

ill in my mind - was the fact that I felt so ashamed of it...' I am babbling now and I know it. I am only going to confuse them if I try to explain things any further. I trail off, mid-sentence.

My daughters, usually so talkative, are now both completely silent in the back of the car. It helps that I can't see their faces, because I am feeling bad enough already.

CHAPTER TWO
The Day Hospital

Soon, we arrive at the mini-roundabout on which
Hahnemann House was built. The old day hospital has
an odd layout, although that never particularly struck me
at the time of my attendance there. The building itself is
huge, Gothic in appearance, with stone steps leading up
to massive double doors. It occupies most of the
roundabout on which it stands, although I know that
there is a small outside space at the back, furnished with
a tiny greenhouse. When I attended the day hospital,
patients were encouraged to undertake a programme of
work in this garden. If they enjoyed it then they would
progress to start sheltered (that is, supervised and
supported) work in a local plant nursery.

I find a parking space in the circular road, directly in
front of the house. I have to look in my rear-view mirror
and then over my shoulder to reverse accurately into the
space, and as I do so I catch a glimpse of two small,
stunned faces with widened eyes. I feel a sharp pang of
guilt. Am I doing the right thing, bringing my daughters
here? It was a wild impulse. I haven't even discussed it
with Paul. But then I didn't need to, I know that. Paul
trusts me with our children. He knows that I always act
with their best interests at heart.

This will be a learning experience, I tell myself now.
The girls will see for themselves what would have taken
me many hours to explain. It will be fine. I am feeling
nervous myself though, at this trip down Memory Lane.
So I take their little hands, one young daughter each side
of me like protective talismans, and the three of us walk
together up those old stone steps, over the threshold of

Hahnemann House.

It is not the same place at all. The Reception area that had stood to the left of the entrance is gone now. I remember dear Pat, who used to sit solidly in that room, dispensing bus money and common-sense. I liked talking to Pat. And she was instrumental in finding me my first real home – her husband was the manager of a local housing association. I didn't expect her still to be there, but I am surprised that there is no longer a Reception at all, no desks or chairs. The large room has been knocked through to the next area, and now there is just one big expanse of space with a bar area and a couple of stools, all empty.

And the wide corridor ahead of us is completely empty too. In the old days there would always be a stray patient or two, standing in the corridor, smoking or nervously pacing or twitching. There would always be an acrid smell of smoke. And at the end of the corridor, behind double doors, there would have been a room crammed with people, almost all sitting numbed and lifeless on a selection of filthy, sagging and torn sofas. Or staring blankly at a television screen, cigarette in hand. Every few minutes somebody would stumble through the double doors, either into or out of that uncannily quiet, yet crowded space. Now there are just closed doors, and silence.

A man approaches us. He is past middle-age but not quite old. A year or two off retirement, I guess from looking at him. He wears civilian clothes, rather than nursing uniform, but has an NHS name badge attached to his shirt. 'David. Charge Nurse,' I read. Ah, so this is still a mental health establishment.

The charge nurse seems surprised to see me and the girls. 'Can I help?' he asks, in a not altogether friendly manner. He probably thinks we are tourists who had wandered out of Bournemouth town centre or off the beach into here by mistake. In response I adopt my best, polite, middle-class voice.

'Um... I used to be a patient here,' I begin hesitantly. I am suddenly beset with doubt. What on earth am I doing here, I ask myself. What am I hoping to achieve with this? 'These are my daughters,' I tell him, once I have gathered my thoughts. 'I want them to see Hahnemann House. Because – uh – I have written a book about it, about my illness, and this place plays quite a major part. I spent quite a long time here, once'.

The charge nurse's hostility dissolves quite quickly. He seems intrigued by my story. 'What is the book called?' he asks with interest, and when I tell him he takes a little notepad and a pen from his upper pocket and notes the title down.

'I wrote the book in my maiden name,' I say. 'Louise Gillett'. I wait for a moment, giving him time to write it down. And then I explain, 'I'm not ashamed any more. It's not embarrassment. That's not why I used a pen name. It's because I don't want my kids to be affected by the fact that I was once diagnosed with schizophrenia'.

He nods. 'Stigma can be a problem,' he acknowledges. I am starting to like this man. He is clearly the sort of mental health nurse who has taken the job for the right reasons. We all walk into the bar area, where the nurse and I stand and chat for a while. The girls stay right beside me. I am glad of that – I am watching them carefully, because I am not sure how much of our conversation they can understand and I don't want them to hear anything that might worry them.

The nurse asks what I think caused my illness, and I reply that I was always a nervous sort of person, but that I believe cannabis played a major part in my downfall. 'Cannabis always does,' he nods. 'Would you know, cannabis features in every set of medical notes I have ever read? Sometimes alone, sometimes as the precursor to heavier drug use'.

This is fascinating stuff. Cannabis use, featuring in every single set of medical notes this nurse has ever seen? I file the information mentally for future reference. I always suspected that cannabis was a far more dangerous drug than many people realise. When I was young, the received wisdom was that it was not addictive, but I was hooked more or less from the first time I tried it. Alcohol, on the other hand, had never tempted me at all. As the child of an alcoholic I knew more about the risks of that particular substance than most, and I was always determined never to let my life be subsumed by it. If only I had known the risks of cannabis use too, I think to myself, not for the first time.

I drag my attention back to the present and try to concentrate on what the nurse is saying. He is explaining that Hahnemann House is no longer a day hospital. Care in the community has taken over completely now, he informs me, and patients are all either visited and treated in their homes by mental health nurses, or seen at clinics. This building is now just offices, although there is still a small cafe area, because some people need a place that they can drop in to, for social reasons.

There is a team of nurses based here, David continues to explain, although almost all of their work takes place outside the building. I glance over to where the nursing office used to be, on the right hand side of the main entrance. Yes, it is still there, still occupied. I still remember the names of the nurses who were so often inaccessible behind that glass door. Anna, Sophie, Richard, Jude... I grew to know them well in the years that I attended Hahnemann House.

A memory flashes – I see myself as a new day-patient, standing outside that door for hours on end, day after day, hoping to speak to one of the nurses. I wince now to recall how pathetic I must have seemed. Whenever somebody finally came to the door, with a sigh that seemed to me to be audible through the toughened and soundproof glass, I never had the faintest idea of what I could say to engage their interest, and so I would stutter and stammer ineffectually, then drift away for a while before taking up my position by the door again. I had sought the company of the nurses partly through loneliness, partly because in those early days I was scared of the other patients and also because I thought that the nurses might somehow have the power to help me, to magically enable me to become strong again.

Snapping out of my reverie once more, I look up and realise that now there are one or two people at the bar counter in front of us, waiting for somebody to serve them with hot drinks. First in line is an old lady with straggly, dyed black hair. She looks unkempt and she is muttering to herself. Behind her stands a much younger man. He is fidgeting, jittery with unspent adrenaline. He pulls a single cigarette out of the pocket of his jacket and put it in his mouth, ready to light once he has got his drink.

Another young man now approaches our small group. He looks skinny - far too skinny - and he smells – there is no polite way of saying this - rank. He has long, straggly, dark hair, rather like that of the muttering lady, who has now retreated to the corner of the room with her cup of coffee. He is dressed smartly though, in a white shirt with black trousers, and he smiles at us kindly. 'Would your daughters like a drink? Or something to eat?' he offers. He signals behind him, towards the bar area, and I feel both girls shrink back against me.

'No thank you,' they say in unison. I am startled. My daughters love food. And drink. They would usually grasp an opportunity like this with alacrity. They are fizzy drink fiends. 'Coca-Cola!', or 'Lemonade!' they always squeal loudly, whenever we take them out to a restaurant.

The unexpected refusal of refreshments reminds me that Anna and Amy are in all likelihood feeling rather unsettled. It is time to go. They have seen and heard more than enough for one day. I am worrying again now, thinking about what damage has been done to them by this visit and I am suddenly grateful that the day hospital has been turned into an admin facility. Seeing the place like this is already enough of a shock for them. A glimpse of the old Hahnemann House might have traumatised them for life, I realise belatedly.

CHAPTER THREE
Schizophrenia

As I drove the car home the girls were much quieter than usual. 'That man was so scary!' they exclaimed. 'The one that offered us a drink. Was he very ill in his mind?'

I smiled. 'You can't always judge people by how they look,' I told my daughters. 'He was a nurse'.

He had worn a badge, which the girls hadn't seen because he had it clipped onto his trouser waistband, making it less noticeable and a bit awkward to read. 'Richard. Nursing Assistant' the badge declared. They had used to be known as Auxiliary Nurses, I remembered. I wondered why it was changed.

I was lost in my thoughts for the rest of the journey until, a short time later, we pulled up outside our house. Actually, although we always called it a house, our home was a two-bedroomed bungalow. Paul and I moved in with Anna when she was only a year old, and we had gradually extended it since then to accommodate our burgeoning family. First we made a bedroom for Anna in what used to be the small study and then we turned the dining room into another bedroom for Amy. The boys still shared a room, but they were happy that way.

Our home occupied a relatively small space, but we made it work for us. The best thing about it was the large garden. Several years before, when Luke was still just a baby, Paul had built what he termed a shed, but which was really a spacious wooden chalet. He built it as a writing room for me, but I had felt guilty having all that space for myself while we were all so cramped inside the house, so I reserved a corner to write in and gave the rest of the space over to be used as a playroom for the children. This worked well – the chalet was easily big enough to accommodate all my books and the overflow of toys from inside the house. We built a conservatory too, from where Paul and I could sit and watch our offspring playing outside, charging around the garden or bouncing on the trampoline. It was our idyll.

I was even more pleased than usual to get home that morning. I needed a cup of tea, and I knew it would not be long before I was inundated with questions. Sure enough, the girls soon came to join me in the kitchen.

'So,' I said, feeling some trepidation, 'What do you want to know?'

'Can we see the book?' asked Anna.

I pulled the cover of the book up on my computer. It was only available online as an e-book. I had published it just weeks previously and it had not yet sold many copies, or got many reviews, so that sometimes I felt as if nothing had changed by my writing it. At other times I realised that everything had changed – my worst fear, of somebody discovering the secrets of my past, had been pre-empted because I had declared those secrets to the world myself. Usually this realisation made me feel surprisingly liberated. At my worst moments, though, I feared that once the book became known, life as I knew it would be over. The information about my past illness would leak out into the community and I would become a social pariah, shunned by friends and acquaintances alike. Local Public Enemy Number 1. The Schizophrenic.

'Surviving Schizophrenia, by Louise Gillett,' Amy read the title of my book out loud.

'That's it,' I said. 'That's what they told me I have. I'm sorry'.

'It doesn't matter at all, Mummy,' Anna told me. 'You were ill once, but you're better now'.

And that was that. The girls wandered off and got on with their day. There was no barrage of questions, no fears or worries to deal with. At first I was taken aback. Perhaps they were still assimilating the information, I pondered. Maybe the fallout would come later.

Then the penny dropped. Of course, I realise. My daughters have never heard or seen the word schizophrenia before. They know nothing about the stigma, the shame of it. They have never heard of mental illness before either, so they don't think that it is any different from physical illness.

I am still just their Mummy, who they love, who was once unwell and spent a long time in hospital. That awful label, which had haunted me for so long, made no more difference to their understanding of me than any other medical term.

If only the rest of the world saw things through such innocent eyes.

CHAPTER FOUR
Dropping another Bombshell

In June 2011, when I published my memoir, it was only available to buy online, as an e-book. This meant that once I had told people of its existence the onus was on them to buy and read it, or not, as they wished. I had no physical copies of the book to hand out to family and friends.

I cared most about my mother's reaction to my book. The memoir was mostly about my childhood, and although I had minimised any mention of my siblings, figuring that their stories were not mine to tell, I had not been able to avoid writing in some detail about my parents.

My father was in some ways the villain of my story, although with the passage of time I had come to realise that no person is all bad or all good, and that everyone behaves the way they do for a reason. In other words, I had long since forgiven him. In any case, he had passed away some years previously, so I had no need to worry about what he would think about the publication of my memoir.

My mother, by contrast, was very present in my life. I loved her dearly and I had always known that she loved me too, and this knowledge had helped me to find a way out of many of the darkest places I had been over the years. I was afraid that my mother would be shaken and hurt by the content of my book, and I really did not want to alienate her.

So why on earth had I risked the breakdown of a

relationship that was so important to me, just for the sake of writing a book about my life? The answer was simple. The writing and publication of my memoir was integral to my sense of self, to my survival. I needed to tell my story.

In any case, it was done now, and I realised that, as with my daughters, I had to tell my mother about the existence of the book before anybody else did. So one afternoon soon after I had published my book online, I invited her over to our house, made her a cup of tea and broke the news. Mum had never been one to show her emotions, and I could read nothing in her expression as she listened to what I had to say.

Of course, she immediately wanted to read the book, so I got my computer and set it up for her on the kitchen table. I found the document and showed her how to scroll the pages up and down, which took a while, due to her sheer panic when faced with the operation of a new-fangled electronic device. And then I left her to it.

As she began to read the words I had written, my mother appeared to sink into them, until soon she seemed to have become attached to the computer screen by an invisible string. She sat immobile on the uncomfortable kitchen chair. The mug of tea I had made for her was gripped in her right hand, suspended mid-air, her elbow angled on the table.

Two hours later, at six o'clock, Paul came home from work. Meanwhile, I had cooked the dinner. I had, of course, asked my mother if she wanted to share our meal, but she refused my invitation with a wordless shake of her head, so we left her at the kitchen table and took our food through to the front room. Dinner over, I headed back into the kitchen, nervously clearing my throat as I gently removed the mug from her hand. It was still full, and the hot drink it had held was now stone cold.

'Would you like another cup of tea, Mum?' I asked. She shook her head again. I was terrified in case she was not speaking to me because I had angered her with my words, and yet I could not help feeling a stab of pride that she was so immersed in my work.

'Er...' I have to go out now, I told her. 'I have to supervise the girls at choir practice. I'm on a rota'.

My mother still did not acknowledge my existence, so I kissed my husband and sons goodbye and left the house with my daughters. As I drove towards the town I couldn't help wondering again how she would feel about me, when she had finished reading. I had written my story with love, but it still laid bare things that my mother had hidden all her life and that I knew she would have preferred to remain unsaid. Things that I had always needed to say, but that she never wanted to hear.

I called Paul from the church as soon there was a break in the choir practice. 'Has she gone?' I asked. Yes, she had just left. 'What did she say? Did she say anything?'

'She just said, 'Well, there's nothing in there that's not true,' my husband told me. 'And then she dashed off. I offered her another cup of tea, but she wouldn't stay'.

So I had no idea how my mother felt. Was she at home now, weeping for the exposure of her past, mourning the loss of her privacy? Was she seething with hatred for the daughter who had betrayed her? As soon as the choir practice ended I drove home with the girls, and I phoned her as soon as I got through the front door. 'What did you think?' I asked. 'I hope you are not too upset'.

To my surprise, she did not seem upset at all; in fact, reading my book seemed to have had a positive effect on her. We chatted about all sorts of family matters, that evening on the phone and also in my home when she came to visit the next day. I felt vindicated – perhaps the memoir would turn out to be as therapeutic for my mother as it was starting to feel for me. With the worst fact of my past exposed – the diagnosis of schizophrenia – I had been prepared for the end of the world as I knew it, but things still seemed to go on almost exactly as they had always done. Perhaps my mother felt the same regarding my revelations of her alcoholism and other aspects of our dysfunctional upbringing. Or perhaps my declarations of love in the book had reassured her, as I had wished them to do. I had never blamed my mother for her shortcomings as a parent and I never would.

In subsequent weeks however, the situation got more complicated. My mother started to worry that people who knew her might read my book and think worse of her as a result. I reassured her that the number of people who had read the book was extremely small, but I still felt guilty and I stopped talking about the book to her.

Several months later, Paul helped me set up a print-on-demand service for paperback copies of the book. I ordered fifty copies for myself, which I sent out for review and gave to some friends, but I didn't give a copy to my mother, or even mention to her that a paperback

edition of my memoir now existed. It was pure
cowardice and I knew it, but I told myself that I was
acting to protect her feelings.

CHAPTER FIVE
Coco

A year earlier, in June 2010, Paul and I had bought a puppy, an eight week old King Charles Cavalier spaniel. As Paul drove the family car slowly home after collecting Coco from the breeder's home I felt maternal and protective, almost as though I had a newly born baby in my charge and not a dog. The puppy nestled into my lap shivering with fear, and I held her close and talked to her in a low voice, trying to comfort her. I couldn't help feeling slightly guilty that we had taken her away from her mother. It seemed odd and somehow wrong that it was possible to purchase such a small, precious life, and I resolved that I would love her and look after her as I did my own children.

The children and I had begged their father for a dog for many years – Anna played the main part in the campaign. Paul resisted manfully, citing his asthma as an excuse, and tried to console the children with a succession of small pets – goldfish, budgies and so on. Then, over the course of one Christmas holiday, when Anna was just eight years old, she became very ill. It was a terrible time for us all. I won't go into the details, but life stopped for a while, and only resumed when Anna was out of danger. To my shame, once we all began to breathe again, I seized the opportunity to get my daughter the thing she craved most in the world.

'Anna could have died,' I said to Paul as we sat together one quiet evening, counting our blessings now that the trauma was over. (The use of the word trauma is not an exaggeration; Anna had undergone two emergency operations in hospital and spent several months subsequently on intravenous antibiotics). 'The least we can do is get her a dog. Just think how happy it would make her'.

It was a dirty trick and I knew it, but it worked. Paul finally gave in to our demands and fortunately he soon grew to love the dog (and nor was his health affected by her fur, as it turned out). In fact, one evening just a few weeks after Coco had come to live with us, I entered the front room to find my husband on his knees on the floor gazing adoringly at our new puppy, who was curled up on the sofa. 'She's so beautiful, isn't she?' she said wonderingly, and I nodded, smiling to myself and biting back the words 'I told you so'.

Coco soon became a vitally important member of our family. There had been some challenging times, physically evidenced by the facts that a) every piece of furniture we owned was either totally destroyed or had tiny teeth marks embedded somewhere on it and b) our house was now completely carpet-free, since we had decided that laminate flooring would be much more hygienic in our new circumstances.

At first the puppy slept in a crate, but after a few weeks that seemed cruel, and we let her sleep in her basket in the front room. Every morning Paul and I would be woken to the sound of screaming, because as soon as the children woke up the puppy wanted to play with them. She played with the four of them in exactly the same way as she would have played with her canine siblings; chasing them around the house and nipping them anywhere she could reach with her tiny, painfully sharp, teeth. Each morning when we heard the shrieks and squeals and got out of bed we would invariably find that the puppy had cornered all four of the children. We would find them standing huddled together on the sofa, quaking and shrieking, because she couldn't (yet) reach them up there.

Catch the children was Coco's favourite game by far, but all the humans in our family were glad when she finally outgrew it.

By now we had taken Coco to training classes, where we'd taught her to stay and sit, and to fetch a ball and return it to us (although only this only happened if she was in the mood). She was pretty much tame, and all of us loved her. Having a dog helped to get us all out of the house more often. We live on the south coast of England, near the beach, and as Coco grew and was able to go on longer walks, a lot more of our time was spent outdoors.

So owning a dog helped our family become healthier and more active. It also helped teach the children to be kinder and more caring – having a dog makes everybody a better person, I am sure. It was especially good to see Luke, the baby of the family, looking after the puppy. I had spoiled my youngest and I knew it – but now the puppy brought out his caring side. Coco scored high all round on the smug mummy factor, if I am to be frank about it.

When I was young we'd always had dogs, but my family did not have a good reputation for caring for them. Our beloved German Shepard dogs Grace and Ghia had been destroyed when I was in my early teens, and my first attempt at owning a dog of my own (when I was in my mid-twenties and already close to a breakdown) had ended in disaster too (I'd handed Ben over to my brother following a long stay in St Ann's hospital after my second breakdown). I had vowed after that never to own a dog again, and I really hadn't thought that I would ever change my mind.

However, my situation had changed vastly over the years – I was in many ways a different person now – and I was determined to look after Coco properly and never to allow any harm to come to her. (Also, looking after a Cavalier King Charles spaniel in a family setting is far different, and much easier, than trying to care for a German Shepard as a young, single, and emotionally fragile woman. I was confident that it would be fine). I knew that I had to forgive myself for all my past failings and shortcomings, and move on with my life.

CHAPTER SIX
Bunions (oh, the glamour!)

The summer of 2011 stretched ahead, full of promise. It was a peaceful time – or would have been, if I hadn't had a bunion operation scheduled for mid-July. Since I was a child, I'd had bunions on both of my feet. Sometime during the previous winter, they had become painful, and recently I has been finding it hard to walk the dog (although I still managed to do so somehow – I needed my daily exercise, which went a long way towards keeping me calm). By early 2011, I was experiencing a stabbing pain in one foot whenever I walked, caused by a corn rubbing on one of my toes. At the grand age of 42 I was starting to feel like an old lady.

One of the other mothers from my children's school was a self-employed chiropodist and she came to my house one day to treat me. I thought that she would just remove the corn and I would be fine, but she was horrified at the condition of my feet. The second toe on each foot had long been bent over the big toes, resting on them when I walked, and these toes therefore had no strength at all in them. 'I don't want to scare you, Louise,' she told me, 'But I have seen old people with this condition who have had to have their toes amputated. You should really get this sorted out'.

Whether or not she had intended it, I was scared. I phoned up the GP to ask for a referral that same afternoon, and within a few months I attended an outpatient appointment at the local hospital. After examining my feet, the orthopaedic surgeon regarded me doubtfully. 'We can remove the bunions and straighten your toes, but I really don't think you should have this operation right now,' he told me. 'It would be impossible for you to recover properly, with young children to look after'.

I insisted that I wanted to go ahead, telling him that Paul would take time off work and I would rest completely for at least two weeks after the operation. I had reasons for this, which I did not share with the doctor. Primarily, of course, I wanted to get the operation over and done with, and prevent any future problems with my feet. But additionally, I had an idea that it might be a good thing for me to be physically out of action around the time that my book was published. Otherwise, I thought, I was in danger of getting over-excited about all that was happening, running around like a headless chicken, and burning myself out. The scheduled operation would ground me – literally.

I was slightly alarmed however, when I realised that the plan was to operate on both bunions at the same time. It really would be hard to do anything at all with both feet out of action, I realised. 'Everyone else I have heard of has had two separate operations, with six weeks to recover in between,' I said to the doctor.

'In your case, this is the way that we are going to do it,' he replied. I had met enough doctors in my time to know that there was no point in arguing.

There was one major consolation – I would far rather have one than two general anaesthetics. I had a deep-rooted fear of anaesthetics and of hospitals in general. In particular, I was scared in case I lost my mind as a result of the anaesthetic. The last breakdown I had suffered, eleven years earlier, was after the birth of my daughter and I had been given pethidine as pain relief. Although I had been very anxious beforehand and had suffered some delusional symptoms during the pregnancy, I suspected that the pethidine had pushed me further towards the edge. I knew that I was sensitive to drugs – cannabis had been a factor in my first two breakdowns, and I kept away from any kind of drugs now, on principle. I didn't even drink alcohol – or only very occasionally and very sparingly. I liked to be in control of my own mind at all times, having been so far out of control in the past.

I really wanted to get the problem with my feet fixed though. I had another motivation – vanity. I had always been ashamed of my unsightly feet and tried to hide them, and now there was a part of me that was very much looking forward to the time after the operation when I would be able to paint my toenails and wear sandals and flip-flops. The fact that I had disliked the appearance of my feet had never been enough to motivate me to get the bunions fixed in the past, but I felt that having pretty feet would be a pleasant side-effect of the operation.

The months building up to the operation were hard. The fear – mostly of the possible effects of the anaesthetic on my mind - began to build. I also had an irrational fear that I would not wake up after the operation. I found it hard not to dwell on the subject, and I wrote about it all at length on my blog. Almost immediately I received support from other members of the online mental health community. One lady, older than me, who had also experienced psychosis told me that even if I did react adversely to the anaesthetic I would be able to stop myself from succumbing to psychosis, because I was aware of the risk. She said that I would recognise what was happening and be able to pull myself back. I hoped she was right.

Early one morning in mid-July 2011, I was admitted to the Royal Bournemouth Hospital for a bilateral osteotomy. I was absolutely terrified on the morning of the operation. Paul took me to the hospital, but then had to go home to take care of the children, so he left me to wait for my turn in the surgery list. The nurses were welcoming and friendly, sending me off to change into a surgical gown and to put my belongings in a hospital locker. I sat trying to read my newspaper in the waiting room with the other patients. I didn't want to think about what was ahead.

After about an hour I was taken up the corridor to meet the surgeon who was going to operate on me. He seemed like a pleasant and capable person, which was a comfort. I confided in him briefly about my mental health history and diagnosis, because I thought that if I should wake up babbling nonsense after the anaesthetic then it would be helpful for the medical team to know why this might be.

Back in the waiting room I struck up a conversation with a lady, several decades older than myself, who was going in to have an operation on her hip. She seemed like a nice sort of person, with a good sense of humour, and talking to her helped me to relax. Soon my name was called to go down to theatre and somehow I managed to hide my fear, lying still as the anaesthetist put me under sedation. He garbled away to his assistant as he did so, and I remember wishing fervently that he would just get on with it.

And then I woke up in the recovery room. At first I was simply relieved to be alive, but then I began to feel quite sick. I told the attendant nurses, who called the anaesthetist. He gave instructions for me to be given more medicine, which he said would stop the sickness but which had an immediately adverse effect. I became suddenly quite panicky, and I experienced a strange and sudden urge to scream out loud. I controlled the feeling, but my mind was racing.

The sickness did not abate but the sensation of panic continued, and I became increasingly suspicious that I hadn't been given an anti-sickness drug at all, but an anti-psychotic. For this reason, when I was asked again how I felt, I told the staff that I was absolutely fine and eventually I was wheeled in my bed from the recovery room back to the ward. Meanwhile, I had become convinced that telling the surgeon about my diagnosis was what had led to this situation. And yet at the same time, I was aware that there was a strong possibility that all this was just advancing paranoia, and that I was descending into madness already.

I was tired and dizzy, and I felt very alone. I knew Paul would be along later with the children, but just now I felt quite abandoned. 'Hello,' a voice suddenly piped up loudly, as though it was right in my ear. 'Hello there'. Oh God, was I hearing voices now?

I was not. Angela, the lady I had met earlier in the waiting room, was waving merrily at me from the next bed. We chatted for a while, and I discovered that Angela used to be a nurse. Gradually, as the effects of whatever drug I had been given wore off, I calmed down.

I was not well physically though – my situation was worse than I had thought it would be. My legs were completely numb from the anaesthetic so I had to be helped to go to the loo (or rather onto the bedpan) which I hated. After that, I put on the hospital radio headphones to distract myself by listening to the radio. To my dismay, I then started to think that the music I heard was sending me messages. I thought, in fact, that the Almighty was trying to talk to me, to comfort me through the music.

I recognised this immediately as a sign of psychosis and I panicked again. I had no intention of telling anyone what I was thinking, though. I didn't want to be given any more medication and I also didn't want to risk being seen by a psychiatrist. I would never forget how, after Scott was born, the psychiatrist sent to assess me in the maternity hospital had insisted that I was mentally ill and should take medication. I had known I was not ill then, but had not dared to disagree. Now, in contrast, I thought that perhaps I was becoming ill – but I didn't want to be given anti-psychotic drugs, or worse, to be carted off to St Ann's. Oh, why did life have to be so complicated? I just lay quietly, tried to be calm, and hoped that my mind would soon return to its normal level of functioning.

Angela struck up conversation again. For some reason, I started to tell her about the book I had just published, although as usual my face reddened and my heart pounded when I brought up the subject. She was shocked, but interested. I handed her my Kindle so that she could read the first section of the book, and she was intrigued.

'You know,' she said, 'As part of my nursing training, I had to work for several weeks in the mental hospital. It was terrifying. We would regularly get attacked with the cutlery in the canteen. It could be fun sometimes, though, especially on Sundays. We used to take all the patients to church, and they would cause havoc, jumping over all the pews, scandalising the congregation…There was one lady who worked as a health visitor,' she went on. 'She was a patient, and she had lived at the hospital for years. She went out to work every day, then came back to the hospital to sleep, because she felt safe there…' She seemed lost in her recollections, but suddenly drew up when she saw my face.

'Sorry,' she said. 'I can tell that you're shocked'.

I was shocked, but I was also fascinated. I listened to Angela reminisce about the mental patients as if they were another species, which I suppose they must have seemed to a young student nurse, fifty or so years ago. They had certainly been a source of interest and amusement. She told me that she had felt in some ways that how the patients were treated was wrong, but that it was just the way things were done. It struck me that in some ways not much had changed. Attitudes were slightly different now perhaps, but some ways of working with mental health patients were so engrained in the system that they would be hard to alter.

Angela was genuinely surprised that I had made a full recovery from psychosis – she hadn't thought that such a thing was possible. Later, Paul came in to visit with the children in the evening, and Angela took great pleasure in watching them, finding them immensely entertaining as they climbed all over me, ate all the grapes and crisps they had brought in and then complained about being bored.

I was pleased to see my family, but surprised by the fact that I suddenly found myself longing for my little dog, Coco. I wanted her undemanding company, and sensed how therapeutic it would be. I knew that if she was with me she would just snuggle quietly onto the bed next to me and I could stroke her. I knew she wouldn't be allowed in but I genuinely yearned for my dog (who usually came firmly second in my affections, after Paul and the children).

I didn't sleep well that first night. The next day Angela went home, as I was supposed to do, but I was hampered by the fact that I could still not move my legs at all. A nurse came and stood at the end of my bed and tickled my toes. 'Can you feel that?' she asked. I could. Then she covered my toes from my view. 'Can you feel it now?' she asked. This time I felt nothing. She explained that the first time I had only imagined I felt her touch because I saw her do so and I was amazed at this evidence of what tricks the mind can play.

I had to resign myself to the fact that I was in hospital for at least one more night. It was a grim night. I could not sleep, although I dozed off fitfully at times. The anaesthetic was finally wearing off, which was a good thing as it meant I would potentially be mobile, but meanwhile the pain in my feet was gradually increasing. I tried to ignore it, but the more I tried not to think about the discomfort, the worse it became. I was upset and increasingly worried. Eventually I gave in, and rang the bell.

When the nurse arrived at my bedside, I told her about the pain and of my inability to sleep. To my horror and despite my protests, she insisted that I take morphine. I was mortified. I told her that I would really rather not take such a strong drug, but she gave me no choice, and watched me closely while I took the medicine.

As soon as the nurse left my bedside, I had a sudden onset of chest pain. I was convinced that I was going to die. I even considered the possibility that the nurse had tried to kill me deliberately. I tried to give the pain a chance to dissipate, but only lasted a few minutes before calling the nurse back to tell her about it. She looked extremely concerned, which I found gratifying. She said that the chest pain was probably a symptom of panic because I had been so reluctant to take the morphine (which did make me wonder why she had been so insistent on administering it against my will). Anyway, to our mutual relief the pain soon subsided.

Paranoia over, I eventually drifted off to sleep for a short while. The next afternoon Paul, with the children in tow, came to collect me. I caught a glimpse in the mirror of the lift on the way down from the ward, and was shocked that I looked so thin, pale and tired. But I had survived. Back at home I slept soundly, and for the next two weeks, Paul looked after me and the children. Gradually, I managed to get up and hobble around the house to do some chores. I found it hard to sit still. I had arranged to share a beach hut during the school holidays with some other families, and as soon as Paul returned to work, by calling in favours from various friends, I managed to get myself down to the beach every day. I hobbled up and down the zigzag paths to the hut, on my crutches and in my black orthopaedic boots. I knew that really I should have just stayed quietly at home, but I had never been good at doing what I was supposed to do.

Once I reached the hut I did sit quietly and let my friends take care of the children, while I guzzled endless cups of tea and chatted. In fact, the sand and sea and the presence of their friends kept the kids happy, so they were no trouble to myself or anyone else. Only Luke, who was only three, came and snuggled up on my lap now and again.

CHAPTER SEVEN
The Alexander Technique

I had prepared for the operation on my feet by losing around seven pounds in weight and by taking lessons in the Alexander technique. I had chanced upon a library book about this therapy, which seemed to present a way to learn to relax and also to help me practice the re-alignment of my body and posture after the operation.

Frederick Alexander was an Australian actor, who lived from 1869 to 1955. In his youth, his voice suddenly failed (a huge problem for an actor, obviously) and his doctors were unable to help him. He found, through a process of trial and error, that this was connected with excess tension in his neck and shoulders, which could be resolved by paying attention to how he stood, breathed and so on. He developed a method to help himself, and later others, to use their bodies in a more efficient way.

Lessons in the technique had to be taken individually, and were pricey, but I decided to go ahead. I found the teacher through an online search, and called to book a lesson. She worked from home, in Poole. I was a nervous driver – I drove around town a lot but didn't like distance driving, so even the ten miles or so to Poole seemed like a stretch.

I had planned out my journey meticulously before I left home, writing down the name of each road and the direction of each turn on a piece of paper. I really was quite a worrier - in stark contrast to my new teacher, who when I finally arrived at her home, struck me as elegant, calm and composed. We talked briefly through my history and about what I wanted to gain from the lessons and then embarked on the therapy itself. It was not taxing - for the first half an hour or so of the session, all I had to do was to lie on a massage table and let the teacher guide my body into the right position for realignment. Later in the lesson I had to sit, stand and walk very slowly, being sure to align my limbs correctly.

I attended six or seven sessions over a few months, and I did indeed feel that the technique had a calming and grounding effect on me. It certainly helped to build up my mental and physical strength prior to the operation. I tried to persevere with the technique afterwards too, but by that time I had started to worry about the cost of the sessions, and so I gave them up.

Anyhow, the summer progressed. Very few copies of my memoir had sold since its publication in June and I often thought that I needn't have even bothered telling my daughters about it. One evening in August, I decided it was time to shake things up a bit. I had already informed family and friends about the book of course, but now I went several steps further.

I fired up the computer, and emailed every single person I knew to tell them about the publication (they would find out anyway, when I was famous, I figured). Paul was shocked, 'I don't think you should be doing that,' he told me, as I clicked the 'send to all' button. I quaked with anticipation of all the shocked and questioning (but supportive) responses. I braced myself for a massive hike in sales and then a lull while everyone I knew read and then mulled over my shocking revelations...
However, book sales remained remarkably low. Fame was a long time coming.

CHAPTER EIGHT
The Church Connection

For a non-religious person (and particularly for one of partly Jewish parentage) I spent a lot of time at Church. I had always liked the local Methodist church. I had met Kate, who ran Mrs Noah's, the church Toddler group, when Anna was young and I had stayed in touch with her over the years. It was Kate who told me about the new monthly Ladies Group at the church. I decided to give it a try - it sounded like a non-challenging sort of activity and it would get me out of the house and talking to people – something I could always do with practice at.

The group was the brainchild of Trisha, the new church family worker. I found Trisha fascinating - she was a tiny vortex of activity, always kind, friendly, and super-open about herself and her life. She was, in short, a lovely person and as I aspired to become a lovely person myself one day, I studied her carefully. The Ladies' Group was called Refine, which I found slightly off-putting. But I liked the meetings, which were much more social than religious. There were usually six or eight of us present. We would chat for an hour or two and then share a short prayer before we went home.

Everyone spoke openly about their lives in these meetings. I soon plucked up the courage to mention my book and the dreaded diagnosis and to my relief everyone seemed to take it in their stride. 'You will have to be careful that other people and their needs for you don't take you away from their children,' Kate advised me. I smiled. I liked the idea of being celebrated and sought after because of my book, but from my recent experience it seemed a highly unlikely outcome. I had been shouting as loud as I could about it for ages and nobody seemed much interested. Which was quite a relief in some ways but still a bit of a blow to my ego.

One evening Trisha arrived at the meeting in visible discomfort. She had just undergone an operation on her back. Her spine had been crumbling, and she had been in constant pain for a long time, although nobody would have guessed. (By contrast, if I have so much as a headache, even my most distant acquaintances get to hear about it). Anyway, Trisha told the assembled group that God had watched over her during her operation. When she awoke from the anaesthetic, she said, out of all the music on her iPod shuffle, the song that played had been the one that meant the most to her, and as far as she was concerned, that literally meant that God was speaking to her.

I marvelled at the coincidence. I too had thought that God was communicating with me after my operation, through the music on the hospital radio! Only I had put it down to lunacy. I wanted what Trisha had… Faith. I wished I could take refuge in faith.

CHAPTER NINE
Grammar School

It was now the beginning of September – eight weeks since the operation. Things were not going well. I had suffered infections in both feet over the summer, and had been prescribed many courses of antibiotics. Every time I finished a course of pills and my wound healed, it immediately swelled up with pus and burst again. It was frustrating, and painful. (What I didn't realise at the time was that I had caused, or at least exacerbated, this problem by sunbathing at the beach all summer with my feet uncovered, in the mistaken belief that the sun would help them heal).

I desperately wanted to be better, and in particular to be able to drive. I'd never had any idea that operating a clutch pedal took any strength, but the first time I had got into my car six weeks after the operation I was incapable of pushing it down at all. I tried again every couple of days after that without success. I had a reason for wanting to drive so badly. Anna had got her place at grammar school, and I wanted to be able to take her in on her first day. Paul couldn't help because he was away in Amsterdam that week, on business. I aired my problem to all and sundry and eventually somebody asked what sort of shoes I was wearing and suggested that a pair with harder soles might help. I tried this and to my delight found that this did indeed make a difference – with tougher soled shoes, I could exert a greater pressure on the pedal.

I felt on top of the world driving Anna to school that first morning, although I was still in some pain. As I approached the school, it felt like a momentous occasion. I had attended the same school myself, more than thirty years previously and although I had not been happy there I was sure that my daughter would fit in perfectly, make many friends and thrive in the academic atmosphere.

We walked together up to the gate, where Anna joined forces with another new girl and left me without a backwards glance. I felt pleased bordering on smug (again) and a couple of weeks later my smugness transmuted into a short manual instructing other parents how they could get their children into grammar school, and why they should do so. It took me two weeks to write about ten thousand words, and I then published my work (with Paul's help) as an e-book.

I loved the ease of self-publishing, and the sense of control. I knew that really I should have written a longer, better researched book but I enjoyed just being able to write the thing off the top of my head and put it out into the world. Two years later when our younger daughter also passed the test, I revised and edited the e-book, adding a couple of extra thousand words. (Yes, I know, still smug).

I decided that I would be quite happy writing and publishing little books like this every couple of weeks. I might earn little or no money, but I would be happily occupied. Unfortunately, my energy and enthusiasm soon fizzled out and I wrote nothing much more for the next six months, except for posts to my blog, and then another short and half-baked tome about successful dieting.

So my writing career was going nowhere fast. On the

other hand, writing and publishing the memoir had developed my interest in mental illness and this started to take over a lot of my time. In 2011, I joined the mental health charity Rethink Mental Illness (formerly known simply as Rethink and before that as the National Schizophrenia Fellowship). It felt like a huge step, after years of hiding my breakdowns and diagnosis from the world, to 'come out' in this way.

And then sales of my memoir suddenly, finally surged at the end of 2011. Amazon developed a new promotional tool for self-published authors, and that was what made the difference. In December, book sales brought in about three hundred pounds in one week. I had never in my life earned so much money in such a short time. I was convinced that this time fame was just around the corner. Of course, I came down to earth again over the next few months, but I was still earning enough money to call myself a writer and start to believe it. As reviews were gradually posted on Amazon, almost all of them effusively positive, I glowed with joy.

CHAPTER TEN
Cognitive Behavioural Therapy

I was still rather a mess personally though – a bundle of nerves and neuroses, in fact. In the early spring of 2012, I embarked on a programme of cognitive behavioural therapy. I had tried CBT twice previously, many years before, without a great deal of success, but I felt that it was worth another go. I hated being nervous, and I was sure that something could be done about it.

The first session did not go well. The therapist told me of her previous counselling experience. She was an ex-psychiatric nurse, and I resented this fact, suspecting that I had been matched with this particular counsellor because of my mental health history, and feeling that this was an example of prejudice. Why couldn't I have a 'normal' counsellor like anyone else, I wondered?

One of the first things the counsellor said was that she wanted me to write down the names of my children, their schools and the doctors' surgery where they were registered. This request made me feel uncomfortable. I told her that I had not come to talk about my children – that they were one thing in my life that I had no problem with and needed no help with. On those grounds, I refused to write down their names.

The counsellor didn't like this. Perhaps she thought it signified a lack of trust in her. She eventually said that it was up to me, but that she would have to 'report' it – which I felt to be an odd use of terminology. I was not a child after all, or a prisoner on probation. I was a human being who had willingly come to her for help. Also, as I told her, I was not keeping my children a secret. They went to state schools, they were well known locally. I just did not want to involve them in my therapy session.

I was not usually assertive, although of course this therapist was not aware of that fact. In any case, the session ended badly. I thought about not going back, but I knew I had to. There was so much at stake – I so badly wanted to be free of my nerves and as I got older I felt that it was even more important to deal with this problem. So I made up my mind that in the next session I would confide in the counsellor. And I did - I told her that my worst fear was of blushing. At the time, uncontrollable blushing seemed such an awful thing to admit to another person – although I had written about it in my book. To my amazement, talking it through made me realise that it was not as much of a problem as I had thought. I stopped caring about it so much – and then it gradually began to loosen its hold on me.

I really was surprised that I was making progress. I needed to let go of a lifetime's worry and anxiety. The counsellor went from being a person who I rather disliked and became somebody I felt I could trust. I realised gradually while I was speaking to her that I had fallen into the habit of worrying about literally everything. While walking the dog I imagined an attacker around every corner. If my children weren't with me I was imagining something awful happening to them. I knew my worries weren't realistic, but they were ever present.

The therapist taught me to practice mindfulness. For example, when walking the dog I began to make the effort to concentrate on my surroundings, rather than let my mind wander into frightening scenarios. I was surprised to find that steadily, rapidly, I became less anxious. One evening I found that I was able to watch the news on television, something I had avoided for years because the stories upset me and preyed on my mind. Now I could watch dispassionately like anyone else – not that I didn't care about what I was seeing, but I wasn't tormented by it. I felt so much happier and more relaxed.

The counsellor did not delve into my history, but if I wished to discuss my past, she listened and offered her thoughts. I came to realise that my character had been shaped in childhood – by my overbearing father, my alcoholic mother, my position as one of the youngest of many siblings, and above all by my own willingness – eagerness, even - always to put myself second to others. I increasingly began to realise that it was possible to change the way I thought about all these things and consequently to change myself.

For so many years I had believed that anxiety was just a part of my personality – now I was discovering that was not true. I started to view the anxiety instead as a problem that had arisen because of past events, a problem which could now be dealt with. This was a revelation.

I was never going to be a perfect person, and I just had to accept that. For example, I knew that I was still over-sensitive. If the therapist yawned in a session I was convinced that she was bored with listening to me (she might well have been, but then again she might have just been tired that day). I knew I needed to stop making assumptions about what other people thought, particularly in relation to myself.

I had developed another worry and I finally blurted it out to the counsellor during the final session of therapy, realising this was my last chance to do so. I had a problem with staring at people, I told her. I stared all the time – I didn't seem able to stop. When I was engaged in ordinary conversation, my thoughts often turned to the fact that I was staring and then I would panic and clam up.

I was sure that this sudden disclosure would stump her, but she took it in her stride. She told me that, as with the blushing, it probably wasn't as noticeable as I thought. She said that every human being looked at others, it was part of human nature. Other people just didn't develop complexes about it. In my case, I knew, the harder I tried not to stare the more conflicted and upset I became, and the more I ended up staring. And I realised, again, that it was the not caring that I needed to cultivate.

The therapist asked if I had ever noticed anyone else who stared in that way, and I told her that I had, many years ago when I used to attend the gym regularly. There was a guy there who couldn't talk to a woman without staring at her breasts. He was well known for it. He even did it to me (despite the fact that my breasts were small and uninteresting and had never attracted much attention from anyone before). She then asked whether I thought any worse of him for his difficulties. I said no, that I had felt sorry for him because he clearly couldn't help himself. She nodded, leaving me to draw my own conclusions.

The sessions were over, and I cursed myself for not having raised the issue sooner. I just had to puzzle it through by myself, armed with the reassurance she had given me. The staring thing had taken over just as the blushing was receding. It was, I realised, almost as though my unconscious, which was used to being in upheaval, needed something to keep it stirred up. Over time, I did learn to deal with the problem by not paying attention to it, by refusing to care.

My worries about staring gradually receded, and when the problem did resurface I told myself that it was a writer thing – all writers are intense. I read somewhere about a scriptwriter being removed from a film set for staring too intensely at the action unfolding before him and thereby distracting the actors. I read too that Picasso pinned people down like butterflies with his stare (but nobody minded because he was brilliant and famous). These stories gave me comfort. It really didn't matter, I told myself. There were many far worse things in life I could have been burdened with.

Changing my thinking habits was hard, but very beneficial. I made more headway in these ten or eleven therapy sessions than in many years beforehand, and far more than in either of my previous two CBT treatments. I supposed this might have been because I had not been open enough with the previous therapists, or because CBT methods had improved, or that this therapist was more experienced, or a better fit for me. Maybe I had just reached a time in my life when I was ready to implement change. Whatever the reason, the results were all good.

CHAPTER ELEVEN
Ghost-Writing

One day my friend Rosemarie asked whether I would be interested in helping a friend of her husband's to write his autobiography. What he wanted, she said, was a ghost writer. I had been asked to help people write their memoirs before, both times, oddly enough, by clairvoyants. I had refused on those occasions, feeling that I would rather get on with my own writing than help others with theirs.

However, this was for a charitable cause. The chap was severely disabled, and he intended to donate all the income from his book to Great Ormond Street and to The Children's Trust. So I agreed to help, and from May 2012 I visited Anton weekly and worked on his book. He paid me for my trouble, and it was good to have a small regular income, although the work was time consuming. It was also a lesson in humility.

I spent about four hours a week on Anton's work. Meanwhile, I was still writing my blog. Through this, I had connected with many other people in the online mental health community and had learned a great deal about mental illness. It was therapeutic to share my experience – and I found that the more I learned about the mental health system, the more disillusioned I became with it.

In ordinary company though, I had to be careful how I expressed my views. One day we visited Paul's brother and his wife. I had recently written in my blog that I was on a mission to abolish the diagnosis of schizophrenia and my sister-in-law had read the blog post and was quite disparaging. She maintained that diagnosis was useful and necessary for medical people because it helped to categorise patients and tailor treatments for them. She told me that I should just concentrate on the fact that I had recovered and help others to do the same if I could, not try to shake up the system.

I found it hard to explain my reasoning. I have never been good with the spoken word. But, I told my sister-in-law, I was starting to feel that all this was increasingly important. It would be different if the diagnosis was based on fact. But it was not – people had been led to believe that schizophrenia was a valid term, but it was no such thing. There was no objective test – it was just decided by observation of behaviour. And the diagnosis had such a huge impact on people's lives. It was all very well me telling people that recovery was possible, but if they were themselves burdened by a label with such negative connotations, told they had a brain disease that was impossible to recover from, why on earth would anyone believe me? They would just assume that I was misguided or had been misdiagnosed, because after all I was not a medical expert, and so many of those who are insist that schizophrenia is an irreversible brain disease.

I could see all this so clearly and it frustrated me that I could not explain it to other people and make them understand. My sister-in-law had some medical training – she was a physiotherapist – and of course she believed what she had been taught about mental illness. But I had personal experience of all this, plus a lot of knowledge that I had garnered on the subject in recent years. I felt strongly that abolishing the diagnosis, or even changing it to a different term, would do so much good to so many people. Since Stephen Fry and Catherine Zeta-Jones had admitted to being bi-polar, the condition was becoming much more acceptable.

And the whole system of diagnosis was based on guesswork, after all. Treatments were often exactly the same for bi-polar disorder, schizophrenia and various other mental health conditions. I knew this for a fact, as the last medication I had taken was Seroquel, and my friend, who had a diagnosis of bi-polar disorder, was on the same drug. Furthermore, psychiatric drugs were very harsh, inexact medicines, and in my experience, they were not very effective. There must be a better, kinder way to help those in emotional distress than by forcing medication on them.

I tried to explain all this, but my problem was always the same - the saner I tried to appear, the more unstable I seemed to be. I have always had trouble expressing myself verbally. I blush, I stammer, I become awkward and make others feel awkward as a result. I fear sometimes that I am not an asset to my own cause – and certainly by the time I left my sister-in-law's house that afternoon I had not managed to convince her of my beliefs regarding mental health treatment.
Unfortunately, I would find this happening again and again over the next few years.

CHAPTER TWELVE
The Schizophrenia Commission

I tried to separate what I thought of as my mental health work (which mostly consisted of writing my blog) and my home life. But early in 2012 I was invited up to London to 'give evidence' to the Schizophrenia Commission. This was because back in November of 2011, when I attended a Rethink Members Day in London, I had met one of the Commissioners, Terry Bowyer, and he had asked me to write a statement for the Commission about my recovery. Having read it, they wanted to hear more from me.

When I had gone to the Members Day, Paul had accompanied me, but this time I had to travel to London alone and I was terrified at the prospect. My daily life for the last twelve years had consisted of no more than toddler groups, the school run and food shopping. This was a massive departure from the usual routine, but I realised that I had to do it. I knew that I was lucky to be invited to this event. The time had come to expand my horizons, and really it was well overdue.

I planned my day in London meticulously. I pored over maps. I packed a large bag with everything I could possibly need, and some things that I knew I would probably have no use for. I checked and double-checked my train tickets (which had been booked and paid for by Rethink). I boarded the train at Christchurch, weak-kneed with fear, and worried all the way to Southampton in case I was on the wrong train. Eventually I plucked up courage to ask a fellow passenger, who told me that I was fine, but should probably change to a faster train at Southampton, which I did. 'I'm sorry to seem so feeble,' I explained, 'But it's the first time I've been to London on my own'.

He smiled at me kindly. 'Oh, an adventure!' he exclaimed and I smiled in return. Yes, I thought, he was right. This was an adventure and from now on I resolved that I would treat it as such, rather than behaving as though it was some kind of unpleasant ordeal. I relaxed further once I had boarded the fast train to Waterloo. I had never used trains much at all in the past, in fact I was not sure than I could remember travelling on one at all. It was a novelty to be able to sit and read a book and think about nothing in particular for such a long stretch of time and I found the experience very enjoyable.

On arrival in London I had to make my way to the King's Fund building. I asked for help again at Waterloo and a kindly guard instructed me on how to buy a tube ticket, probably wondering to himself how a middle-aged woman could possibly be so green behind the ears. So I eventually found my way to my destination, feeling very excited to be in the centre of London alone. Perhaps I was more capable than I had thought, I reflected. This didn't seem to be so very difficult after all.

There were about thirty people at the Schizophrenia Commission meeting. We split into groups and spoke amongst ourselves about recovery. I found myself becoming very nervous, and speaking too much as a consequence. I found the stories of the others in the group very interesting though. One chap in my group spoke about how he used the opportunity to educate himself while he was recuperating from his illness – he took as many courses as he possibly could. Another woman was still on medication and said that she seemed to break down whenever she stopped taking it.

The health editor of The Independent was one of the Commissioners in our group. It transpired that he knew the author Jeanette Winterson. I spoke to him about her book, 'Why Be Happy When You Could Be Normal?' She had revealed in that book that she heard voices, I said, and he told me that yes, she did still occasionally hear voices when she was stressed or worried. I was extremely impressed with her bravery in admitting to it, and thought that it would do a lot of people good to know that such a successful person had such a symptom (hearing voices, or auditory hallucinations, is supposed to be a classic symptom of schizophrenia. I do not personally suffer with it. However, many people who are not mentally ill also hear voices. This is one of the many things I have learned over the past few years).

Another Commissioner in our group was a psycho-pharmacologist. He said that he had recently been diagnosed with high cholesterol and was given statins. He was determined though, not to take them, and instead he had tackled his diet and exercise regime and found the remedy there. I told him that I had done the same thing, and that I was disappointed that others with my diagnosis were often not given the freedom to stop their medication and find their own route back to wellness. He seemed very interested in this, as if it was not a possibility that had occurred to him before.

At lunchtime, I spoke at length to a Commissioner called Alison Brabban. She was a kind person, and seemed very knowledgeable. It turned out that she was a psychologist. I told her about my frustration with the diagnosis, and she was very supportive. I asked whether there was a possibility I had been misdiagnosed. Otherwise, how was it that I could managed my life without medication while others could not? Alison said, very emphatically, that I had had schizophrenia, but that I had recovered. She was extremely scathing of those psychiatrists who said recovery from schizophrenia was impossible.

I also spoke to Sir Robin Murray, the Chair of the Commission. I told him that it was good of him to be open-minded about mental health and he said at his age he had to be open-minded, which didn't make any sense to me, but I nodded and smiled as if I understood exactly what he meant.

So I had networked as much as I was able and certainly more than I had ever done before in my life. The day was soon over and Clare Gerada, another Commissioner, who at the time was Head of the Royal College of Physicians, summed up by stating that the diagnosis of schizophrenia was a barrier to recovery. I travelled home exhausted but elated, feeling that I had been instrumental in effecting a really important change. I was sure, from what I had heard and experienced during the day, that the Schizophrenia Commission Report would recommend abolition of the diagnosis.

CHAPTER THIRTEEN
Raymond Briggs

Time passed. I had an income from my writing now, and I gradually starting to feel that I was moving forward with my life. One day soon, I felt sure, I would really feel like a writer.

One afternoon in July 2012 I was just about to leave the house, on my way to Scott's school play. I noticed a letter on the doormat, and picked it up. It was addressed to me in lovely copperplate handwriting and looked more interesting than any correspondence I had received for a while. I opened it quickly, hardly able to believe my eyes as I scanned it greedily.

'Many thanks for your superb book. Absolutely brilliant. Fast-moving and unputdownable'.

I drank in the words greedily. It was a long letter – two pages. The first part of the letter praised my book. The second part listed all the great writers and artists who had been 'mad'. It went on to say, 'Just started your book of poetry. Read the first two. Brilliant again, and funny'.

I had almost forgotten writing to Raymond Briggs, the author of The Snowman, a month or two earlier. I had sent him a copy of my book, and hoped he might reply, but I certainly hadn't been expecting this.

I was stunned, and I couldn't stop grinning to myself as the impact of the letter sunk in. A proper author – a really good writer and artist – had read my book and loved it! I took the letter with me to the school play, and showed it to my friend Jackie, who already knew all about my memoir because she had proof-read it for me. (Not all the school Mums knew about the book, or if they did know, then I didn't know that they knew. Confused? Me too).

Later that even, after I had shown the letter to Paul, I tucked it away inside my copy of Ethel and Ernest. Raymond Briggs had signed that book for me some years ago, during one of the darkest periods in my life…

It was January, 1998. I was in Brighton for a weekend with my then-boyfriend, Mark. We had stayed the previous night in the Grand Hotel, which had cost just twenty-five pounds, including breakfast the following morning. The reason for this was that over Christmas I taken a position as a chambermaid in the Royal Bath Hotel in Bournemouth. It was a horrible job (the place was infested with cockroaches) but there was one consolation. Employees could stay in other hotels in the chain at discount prices and so I had 'scored' a room at the Grand Hotel.

As Mark and I mooched around Brighton we passed a bookshop and I glanced in the window. I saw a poster advertising the fact that Raymond Briggs was due to be signing books there soon. I checked the date of the signing – it was today! And then the time – it was right now!

Raymond Briggs had long since been one of my literary heroes. I had recently read his wonderful picture book, Ethel and Ernest, and learned that his late wife had suffered from schizophrenia. I had also happened across an article in Woman and Home magazine in which he talked about her illness, and consequently I felt that he and I had something in common.

Shaking with excitement, I picked up some books and joined the end of the author signing queue. Mark was not interested in queuing so he went off to a nearby coffee shop, and I arranged to meet him later. I was right at the end of the line, and increasingly nervous as I drew closer to the front of it. When my turn arrived, I handed over the three or four books that I was holding, and while he was writing in them, I falteringly spoke to Raymond Briggs.

I told him I had read about his late wife and that I had been diagnosed with the same condition. He was surprised, telling me that I looked well. (I did look well at this point, I suppose. I had stopped recently stopped taking psychiatric medication, under medical supervision, because I desperately wanted to have a child. Mark and I were due to get married. I had lost the extra weight that I was carrying since my last breakdown, and I was exercising regularly in order to get as fit as possible).

I told the author that I had read about his wife in the magazine interview as well as in his book. He took a real interest and we spoke for what felt like ages. I told him that I dearly wanted a family, and that I was not currently taking medication for that reason. He told me that the psychiatric medication his wife had taken had killed her. Then he seemed to realise what he had said, and reassured me that, 'The drugs were much worse in those days'. He also told me that he tried to help the NSF (the organisation that later became Rethink) whenever he could.

I was touched by his kindness and by the time he took to speak to me. He didn't seem to be in a hurry at all, although he must have been tired. I was on cloud nine when I left the bookshop, and walked down the road, clutching my newly signed books. Then realised that I had not paid for any of them. Horrified as well as flustered now, I returned to the shop, explained myself and paid up, still overcome by the excitement of what had happened.

Anyhow, that meeting was why I had thought to send Raymond Briggs a copy of my book. And he loved it! Raymond Briggs! Loved my book! I would never need any further affirmation of my talent in my life, I vowed. Raymond Briggs believed that I was a gifted writer. It would always be enough.

I had also sent a copy of my memoir to Virginia Ironside, the agony aunt and author. There was history here too - many years before, I had entered a competition in Virginia's column in the Independent newspaper. The challenge was to answer a reader's problem. I did so, and I also sent a letter to Ms Ironside, telling her about my own personal worries and difficulties (I had mostly wanted her advice about my alcoholic mother). She replied with a long letter of advice, which I still treasured. And this time, when I sent my memoir, she also took the trouble to reply, by email. She praised my writing and said that the book told a fascinating story, although she wasn't sure about the fact that I had decided to write it in the present tense ('the influence of Arvon, I suppose', she had written, a trifle testily).

I don't remember exactly who else I sent a copy of the

book to, but I do know that not all of them took the trouble to reply (and I tried very hard not to resent this, because I really am not an egomaniac). I know I sent a copy to Robyn Bolam, who was a lovely person – I had met her once at a poetry group meeting. She was a Fellow of the Royal Literary Society and a well-known poet, librettist and academic. She wrote a glowing review of my memoir on Amazon, as did Clare Allan, a journalist at The Guardian and author of a wonderful book called 'Poppy Shakespeare'. (By the way, do read Poppy Shakespeare if you get a chance. It is a staggeringly good book – funny, but also moving, and it manages to be scathing about the vagaries of the mental health system without being judgemental. All this, wrapped up in a really good, page-turner of a fictional story).

CHAPTER FOURTEEN
Dealing with Criticism

The final draft of my memoir had been written in a frenzy, over about nine months. It had been a long time brewing though – various drawers and cupboards in my home were still stuffed with manuscripts of the book, all slightly different. This final version was a fourth or fifth draft. And now I discovered that creatively I was stuck. I wanted to keep writing, but I knew that my first book had taken me literally years to write. In some ways, it was the work of a lifetime. How could I beat, or even equal, that? And I felt that I should beat it, that I needed to write something better. It was no use following a good book with a worse one, I told myself. I set myself high standards and as a result I became paralysed with the fear of failure.

I knew that I was not alone. Anyone who has written a successful first book worries about how to better it, and quite a few writers become blocked as a result. But a year passed, then more, and then something happened which upset me. I was approached by a friend who took it upon herself to inform me that 'local people' thought I was doing the wrong thing, publishing a book about my mental illness. Apparently, the prevailing opinion was that it would adversely impact on my children. This hurt me deeply. Surely, I thought, anyone who knew me at all must know that I always put my children first. Surely people must realise that I had not taken this course of action before considering any effect on them very carefully indeed.

I rarely wrote about the children in my blog. If I did, it would make it much more interesting – just as this book would be a much more entertaining tome if I wrote more about my family life in it – but I don't want to use my kids for my own purposes. However, conversely, I cannot deny their existence in my writing. My children are a large part of my life. They are the source of my recovery, my well-spring.

I didn't usually speak up in my own defence when I was hurt or upset (usually I just stayed silent and expressionless while thinking bitter thoughts, a trick I had perfected during my various sojourns in St Anns. I must have been good at it, because they labelled it 'catatonia' there). I couldn't help retaliating this time though. 'Actually, I think it will do my children good to know that their mother feels able to be open and honest about her life,' I told my critic. 'After all, there is nothing for them to be ashamed of. I have never harmed anybody, I have only ever been ill'. Later, I poured my heart out in my blog, something that always helped me to reason through my actions.

I had the best of intentions in writing the book, I wrote. Hopefully the benefits to others would justify the personal risks I had taken. Hopefully my children would grow to understand. Anyone who thought worse of them for anything that I had suffered was not worthy of their company. The writing flowed, and by the time I had finished I felt calmed and reassured. If only I could write another book as easily as I wrote those blog posts, I thought.

So my writing had stalled, and my confidence was fluctuating, but meanwhile I was busy at home. Luke, my youngest child, was now at playschool. He went for five mornings a week and I usually used those hours to walk the dog, shop and clean the house. The rest of the time I spent with him, often taking him out to toddler groups or friends' houses. Then at three o'clock the other children returned from school and after the snack time frenzy I would embark on cooking the dinner. My life was overrun with mundane tasks, and soon enough I began to wonder how I had ever found time to write a book in the first place. My life was all about looking after Paul and the children, and that was just how I wanted it, I told myself.

CHAPTER FIFETEEN
A New School Year

Then, in September 2012 Luke, our youngest, started full-time school. Now I really had some free time, and I could not convince myself otherwise. I could get on with my writing in earnest. But instead, I filled up my free time with various small tasks in and outside the house. I was already busy for one day a week with Anton's book, and I then embarked on another major commitment, a Psychology A level, which took up another day a week.

One afternoon a week, I volunteered to help with reading at school, in Scott's class. Next I set up a writing group in the local village hall - we met every Friday morning. I ran the group on behalf of the charity Rethink, and I took no payment for doing so. The group ran smoothly from the start, although attendance was sometimes quite low.

I met some fascinating people through that group. I really liked one elderly chap, who had been diagnosed with schizophrenia as a young man and had taken medication his whole life. He was a lovely man, who had worked as a teacher, and was married with two children and a grandchild on the way. The only symptom he seemed to suffer from was insomnia, but he had never questioned the diagnosis and indeed seemed to be very grateful that psychiatrists had uncovered what was wrong with him. In fact, he had such incredible faith in the medical profession that I am sure he would have willingly agreed to a lobotomy if he had been told that it would benefit his health. All of which I supposed was fine, as long as he was happy.

CHAPTER SIXTEEN
The Schizophrenia Commission Report

So I spent the academic year from September 2012 ghost-writing, studying psychology, helping at the nearby Junior School and running a writing class. I had also been busy with the occasional mental health event. Late in the summer of 2012, when the Schizophrenia Commission report was almost ready for publication, I was asked to write a 'case study'. Basically, I had to put together a couple of hundred words saying what I thought was important in an examination of the current mental health system.

I had strong opinions about the mental health system. Over the previous years, as I wrote my blog and communicated with other bloggers and activists, I had realised that there was a whole network of people who had experienced adverse effects from the mental health system and felt strongly about the need for reform of it. I had come to feel particularly strongly about several matters. For example, I learned that anti-psychotic medication did not work in the same way that patients were led to believe, that there was no actual proof of the 'brain disease' schizophrenia. I had also begun to recognise that the most serious damage I had suffered personally came from believing that I was 'schizophrenic' – the label itself did untold damage and actually stood as a barrier to recovery (as Clare Gerada had summed up at that meeting at the King's Fund Building).

So now I leapt at the opportunity to expound my views about diagnosis and forced treatment, in writing. In my statement I made it clear that in my opinion the diagnosis had to go, because it was causing more harm than good. A couple of weeks later, I received an email from Rethink, who were dealing with the administration of the Commission's work. The email said that the part of my statement which dealt with diagnosis was not really relevant and should not be published.

All my life, I had been in the habit of complying with anything that anybody ever asked of me. I was that sort of a person. I wanted to help, and I wanted people to like me. This time though I reacted differently, although only after thinking the matter over for several days. I emailed back, saying that if they wanted to use my case study at all, they could not dispense with this central part of it.

I was very pleased when they acquiesced with my request, and my view about diagnosis was left in the Report. I was astonished though, that they had wanted to change it in the first place. What was the point of asking for people's opinions and then trying to censor them? And in light of all this, it now looked pretty certain that the Schizophrenia Commission had no intention of recommending abolition of the diagnosis. It was a devastating realisation.

CHAPTER SEVENTEEN
Growing Up

Thank goodness, my home life took up a lot more space and time in my life than my mental health 'work'. Everything was ticking along nicely at home. I was very lucky with all my children – they were healthy and happy and just being in their company gave me great joy, The only real problem Paul and I had come across (apart from Anna's spell in hospital in the winter of 2008/9) was Scott's speech disorder. Our two girls had been articulate from an early age, but when Scott first began to speak his words had been pretty much unintelligible, however hard he tried to make himself understood.

He was diagnosed with dyspraxia, and embarked on speech therapy when he was just three years old. He had to learn to pronounce each sound separately, painstakingly, and for many years he made slow progress. I found it very stressful. But Scott had always been very patient and stoic about it all and now he was gradually growing out of the problem. One day on a short break at Center Parcs in Longleat, we stumbled across a person dressed up as a giant Rupert Bear character, having a tea party in the grounds for the children.

Scott regarded this scenario for a moment, and then turned to me. 'Mummy,' he said, with a serious expression on his face, 'That bear makes me feel oddly uncomfortable'. I will always remember that moment - it marked a turning point for me. I could understand most of what Scott said by now, but he rarely communicated his thoughts. He only asked for what he needed, never tried to say anything complicated or unnecessary. I suppose it had always been too much trouble to make himself understood.

So I was very glad to hear that Rupert the Bear made Scott feel oddly uncomfortable when he was eight years old, and I have never forgotten the look on his face when he told me about it. (In fact, he turned out to have picked up an amazing understanding of vocabulary and syntax from all those years of quiet listening – one day, a few months later, when he started a cold he said, 'My nose is troubling me').

I had not remained entirely anxiety-free since my sessions with the counsellor. My agitation crept back sometimes. Fortunately, I was usually able to take steps to stop myself getting overly stressed. I would cut down on caffeine for a while, or increase the amount of exercise I took, to get my sleep patterns straight. I always felt better after a good sleep. And the benefit of the counselling did stay with me – I was always aware now of when I started to worry, whereas previously anxiety had just seemed to be a permanent part of my life, something that I usually failed to notice happening.

I had created an environment for myself – a family environment – where I felt valued, accepted and content. This, I knew, was the main reason that I had recovered so well from my past breakdowns – and because I had learned how to look after myself I was almost certain that I was not going to break down again. I had 'blips' – times when I would get upset with one thing or another – but at these times I told myself that it was normal to be upset sometimes, that mood swings were not a sign of anything sinister and that every human being has ups and

65

downs.

I did have serious concerns about Anna for a while after she read my memoir. She is a voracious reader and has always been very mature. She had been asking to read my book for a long time and eventually I gave in. She was only twelve years old at that time, and I was well aware that the content of my book might upset her, but I thought that if I was on hand to talk to her about it as she read then I could deal with her concerns as they arose. Afterwards, though, I realised that I had miscalculated the situation badly. I hadn't realised exactly how much my daughter had idolised me, and unwittingly I had taken myself right off that pedestal very suddenly and finally.

I hated the thought that my daughter was disappointed in me, and I really regretted letting her read the book. Her disillusion was difficult for us both to cope with. However, I was aware that the best tack was to be consistent and offer reassurance and gradually Anna adjusted to her new notion of me, although she did develop a degree of embarrassment about the existence of the book. (Thank goodness, she has finally got over than now, two years on. But I have learned my lesson. Amy is twelve now, and I shall definitely wait many years more before I let her read my memoir – not that she shows any interest in doing so).

Once every few months I was invited to a mental health event, usually in London. I welcomed these diversions, although they always seemed to follow the pattern that was set when I gave evidence to the Schizophrenia Commission. I became over-stimulated and over-talkative, tried too hard to get my points across, and by the end of the day I would always feel exhausted and demoralised. I was always pleased to be invited to these events, and I often met interesting people who furthered my understanding of mental health, but I never really felt that I was contributing much of value to the debate. I just kept repeating my opinions about diagnosis and forced treatment, hoping that at some point something would change as a result.

CHAPTER EIGHTEEN
Newcastle University

I was still marketing my memoir, and some money was still coming in from sales, although things were gradually slowing down. One day, in the autumn of 2012, I received a message on Twitter from a lady who said she had read my book and wanted to get in touch. She turned out to be the public engagement officer from Newcastle University and told me that she wanted me to go there to give a talk about the book to Psychology staff and students. She said I would be paid well for my time and of course I accepted her invitation with alacrity.

The University were putting on an art exhibition, which had been planned for some time. The exhibition, by the artist Susan Aldworth, was called Re-Assembling the Self. My talk would be one of the ancillary events set up around this exhibition. I was beside myself with excitement, but also terrified. I prepared the talk meticulously. I went shopping and bought a smart outfit, and even had my hair blow-dried the day before my journey. I caught the train to Southampton Airport with hours to spare, and waited in the passenger lounge at the airport still full of nerves, but with a burgeoning sense of my own brief importance.

When I arrived in Newcastle, I took a taxi to the hotel. I couldn't remember the last time I had used a taxi. I had certainly never been in one alone. A room at the Hilton Hotel had been booked for me, and by the time I reached my room my head was as inflated as it had ever been. It was not long before my ego was punctured by my increasing panic though as I unpacked, dithered about a bit, practised my speech for one last time in front of the mirror in my room and then took a taxi to the University.

Kate, the Public Engagement Officer, had asked me to meet her for lunch on campus. We met in a café, surrounded by chattering students, and although food was the last thing on my mind, I managed to eat a meal extremely slowly as we talked. Suddenly lunch was over. There was not much time now to be fearful. I followed Kate through the maze of University buildings which led to the one my talk would take place in. I noticed that there were posters along the walls advertising my talk, and I stopped to take a picture of one, to show to Paul and the children later. My name, on a poster. Fame at last!

The lecture hall was a small one and it was not full. There were about thirty students present, and a few older people who I thought might be lecturers. I started by reading a poem I had written about schizophrenia. I had wondered if this was a good idea initially – might it make me look a little off the wall? But then, I reasoned, I had a diagnosis of schizophrenia. I could behave exactly how I wanted, and nobody could possibly think any worse of me.

Luckily, the audience seemed to enjoy the poem. I moved on to the talk. Anna and Amy had helped me prepare a slideshow to illustrate my points. I spoke briefly of my own experiences, but mostly about how I believed recovery from serious mental illness could be achieved.

Afterwards, I invited questions from the audience. Most of these questions are lost to me now, but I do remember one student asking, 'What would have helped?'

'Not just during hospital,' she elaborated. 'Because obviously while you were there, and afterwards, you didn't get the attention you needed, the right sort of attention. It was only much later, when you decided to give yourself that attention, you began to recover. But what would have helped, what could have been done differently by the mental health services?'

I told her, and the assembled group, that I would not have had my life any differently. I could see now where I had made some wrong choices, but at the time I didn't know that. And now I had learned so much from my experiences that I didn't regret any of them – although I wouldn't have wished that suffering on anyone else.

Straight after my talk, Kate took me along to another author event. At this event, Patrick Cockburn read extracts from the book he had written with his son, Henry. The book was called, 'Henry's Demons'. I had read it several months previously, and found it fascinating. After the event, the audience were given the opportunity to ask questions.

Henry, like me, had a diagnosis of schizophrenia. I was keen to know how he felt about this label, so I asked him, and was astonished by his response. Henry told me that he was, 'Proud to be schizophrenic'. I could not understand it and was too stunned to question him further, but later I pondered his attitude. I really had no idea why anyone would profess to be proud to be schizophrenic.

I have thought about it since, and all I can surmise is that perhaps for Henry the label signalled to the outside world that he should be left alone, that he was a hopeless case. Perhaps to him, the label bought some element of peace. He would certainly never recover from his illness if he embraced that definition of it, I thought sadly. But then I pulled myself up – I knew that I needed to realise that it was not up to me to save others. Particularly those who did not want to be saved. I had to stop assuming that it would be better if everybody else thought the same way as I did, or that they could be persuaded to see things my way.

That evening, Kate had booked a local restaurant for some members of the University staff, and for Susan, Patrick, Henry and myself. I sat next to Patrick, and we talked about various things, including my desire to be accepted as a writer. We didn't talk about the subject of schizophrenia at all. I had read Patrick and Henry's book, but they had not read mine and I was quite pleased about this in a way, because I felt that our perspectives on the problem were so different that it might have made the meeting awkward.

I very rarely drink alcohol and that evening was no exception. That night, though, I slept fitfully as I often do after social events. The evening played back over in my mind as thought it was on a video with a constant, tedious, loop. Had I made a fool of myself in any way? Had I talked too much, or not enough? Sometimes, my brain was just too active for its own good.

The next day I journeyed home. I was tired, and my mind kept returning to that student's question after my talk. 'What would have helped? What could have been done differently?' the girl had asked. I hadn't answered her properly, I realised now. I had said that I wouldn't have wished things to be any different for me – but what she had wanted to know was how the mental health system could be altered in such a way as to help others, to alleviate their suffering. It was a subject that I kept turning over, again and again in my head… What would have helped?

CHAPTER NINETEEN
Rethink Members Day 2012, Nottingham

I travelled to Nottingham with my friend Julie for this event, where the Schizophrenia Commission Report was presented by Sir Robin Murray. As I had suspected, the validity and usefulness of the diagnosis was not in dispute. Instead, Sir Robin spoke for some time about services and attitudes to mental illness, and the longer he went on, the lower my heart sank correspondingly. All I could hear was a lot of empty talk and some proposals to fiddle around the edge of the system.

Anyhow, the day was soon over and Julie and I headed home. I was drained again, both emotionally and physically and I wondered as I always did why I continued to attend mental health events. Of course it was because I wanted to learn about mental illness and to communicate with others who had been through similar experiences to my own. But I always felt that such events drained my own health, detracted from my peace of mind and somehow set me backwards.

I had got better, moved on with my life, by dismissing all thoughts and memories of my breakdowns, so why, I asked myself, did I now persist on this path of uncovering and examining them? It was a compulsion and I convinced myself it was for good cause, but I was beginning to realise that there was a strong possibility that all my grandstanding was pure self-indulgence, something that had grown from the need to feel important.

And so I kept on shifting from the shadow world of mental health to the world of light and laughter at home and back again. I played with my kids and enjoyed my comfortable, wholesome life. And then I plunged back into the examination of mental illness, its causes and its solutions. I couldn't help feeling that if I thought and wrote about it for long enough I must come up with some answers.

Meanwhile, I had to keep the house clean and tidy, walk the dogs, and be at the beck and call of the family. If the children were ill, of course, I had to drop everything and stay at home to look after them. I felt privileged not to have to work outside the home and I wondered how on earth anybody could hold down a job, with this sort of pressure. I still wanted to write more books but had filled up my time so much with other activities that I had no opportunity to do so. At least, I consoled myself, I was still able to contribute to the household from the proceeds of my first book and the money that Anton was still paying me each week to put his autobiography together.

I was enjoying the Psychology course. However, when the first exam came around, in January 2013, I felt completely unprepared and began to panic. I told myself I had no need to take the exam since I didn't need another academic qualification – but then I pushed through and sat it anyway. Anna helped me to revise, and she was very patient and calm about it all, which helped immeasurably.

The other members of the class knew about my diagnosis by now, because I had decided during one lesson to 'confess' to it. My heart was beating fast as I broke the news. The others were surprised and initially fascinated, and we had some good discussions around

74

the subject. It turned out that one of the other students had also had a breakdown and a stay in St Ann's. Her experience was very different from mine – she had received good therapy and felt strongly that the hospital had helped her.

I thought at first that the difference in her attitude to St Ann's was because her breakdown was more respectable than mine. Her illness was triggered by a physical event, an accident, whereas mine was just because of an inherent weakness in my mind (or perhaps because of cannabis and stress and so on. But there had been no one precipitating event for me). Plus, I reasoned, she didn't have 'The Diagnosis' so she had never experienced the shame I had on that count.

On reflection, though, I began to wonder whether a lot of the reason that my friend had a more positive experience was because she accepted her treatment instead of resenting it. She had gone into hospital voluntarily and been grateful for the help she had received, in sharp contrast to the unpleasantness of my incarceration and forced treatment and my consequent resentment of the whole experience.

Trust, I concluded, was the key. Trust was invaluable. The main, the most important change in the mental health system would be if it could be transformed into a service that people believed would help them. (This has already happened in Northern Finland, where schizophrenia has basically been eradicated – almost everyone with a first episode of psychosis never relapses. In a Daniel Mackler film set there, he posed the question to patients, 'Do you trust the system to help you?' and the unequivocal answer was yes. Here in the

UK, unfortunately, the mental health system has the potential to be brutal, and as long as that brutality remains, it will never be a service that is worthy of trust).

In any case, my Psychology classmates were kind and inclusive and I never felt shunned as a result of the things I had divulged. However, over time, I did feel their interest falter as I became progressively more worked up about what I perceived as the faults in the exam syllabus. I was constantly infuriated that A level students were still being taught that 'schizophrenia' is a brain disease. The others in my class had lost interest in the subject and wanted to move on, which was understandable. Their lives weren't at stake, after all. They hadn't been de-humanised by being termed 'schizophrenic'. They just wanted to pass the exam.

The second part of the Psychology exam was in June, and again I had to brace myself for it. I was petrified of failure. For a second time I almost bottled out. I told myself that the qualification was of no use to my future and that it would be better not to put myself through the stress. An additional problem was that for this exam I had to 'learn' several things I knew to be untrue – not just about schizophrenia, but things such as how depression is caused by low levels of serotonin. (This is widely accepted as fact but has never been scientifically proven). So I told myself that the exam was all wrong anyway, that I didn't want or need to learn and regurgitate facts that I didn't agree with. But I knew all along, really, that I would take the exam. I always push through. I always force myself to do the things I find difficult. And so I duly knuckled down to my studies and took the exam, keeping my sense of integrity intact by liberal use of the phrase, 'It is thought that…'

I was really pleased when the A level results came out in August, and I found that I had got a respectable B. I was extremely pleased to discover that my grey cells were still working. I declined the opportunity to study for another year to get the full A level though. A psychology AS level was enough for me to feel that I had proved a point. I resolved to cut down on my commitments for the year ahead and concentrate on my writing.

So as soon as the course was finished I stopped volunteering to help at Scott's school. Anton's book was almost completed now. My commitments were reducing rapidly. The one thing I did continue with was the writing group, which was no longer affiliated to Rethink, and which had moved from the village hall to the library. There were about eight of us, although attendance fell off on occasions. I didn't want to stop the group because I had found that it helped me to get into the habit of writing and freed me up creatively. In the company of other writers I stopped worrying so much about the quality of my writing and concentrated instead on simply putting words on the paper. It was starting to be fun again – which of course, is the whole point!

CHAPTER TWENTY
A Meeting with the Department for Work and Pensions

One day in the summer of 2013 I was invited to an event at the Rethink offices in London. I was particularly relaxed that day, as I travelled up on the train and then walked slowly up the Thames Embankment to the Rethink building. I had been there several times now. I remembered the first time I had been to London alone, to the Schizophrenia Commission meeting at the Kings Fund Building, how crippled I had been by my nerves, and marvelled at how routine I now found this journey in comparison.

This meeting was on the subject of how to get people who had been seriously mentally ill back to work and there were about fifteen or twenty 'experts by experience' present. I was convinced that properly paid work helped people to recover and I told that to the civil servants present. I also told them how hard it is when you are on disability benefits, because you don't want to risk losing them by trying to work, in case you fail and then find yourself mired in poverty again, with all the attendant stress. But, I said, I had only considered myself to be fully recovered in the last two years since I had been off benefits. Work had been crucial to regaining my self-esteem and recovering my sense of self.

The civil servant at our table was a lovely lady, very calm and dignified but also understanding and I mentally added her to my list of role models. I told her about my memoir and my frustration with the diagnosis of schizophrenia, and she said something very interesting in return. She told me that through her work she had met Lord Wolfenden, whose 1957 Report had effected huge change in the law on homosexuality. And Lord Wolfenden himself had said to her, when she congratulated him on work well done, that, 'Change is of the time'. In other words, change will come when it is the right time and agitating for it really makes very little difference. Wise words, indeed.

Around this time, I finally finished my work on Anton's autobiography. My friend Jackie put a lot of work in to proofread the book, as she had done for my own paperback. The final version was not how I would have wanted it – I felt it was too long, not pithy enough. I would have dramatized it, edited it a lot. But it was the book Anton wanted, and so I had to take my ego out of the picture. That was a valuable lesson for me, as was the fact that this book had come along slowly and methodically.

By sticking with it, week after week, with hardly a break, a thousand or a couple of thousand words each time, Anton and I had gradually produced a book – a long book. It was a revelation to me. My memoir had come along after years and years of writing and many, many rewrites. This one was much quicker, in terms of actual hours put in. Something clicked for me then – if I just wrote a few thousand words each week, I realised, I should have another full-length book of my own ready after roughly a year.

CHAPTER TWENTY-ONE
National Psychosis Summit, April 2014

Life was a whirlwind – with four children, there were always things to do, places to go with them. I didn't want to miss a minute of them growing up. I knew that having a family was the most important part of my life, and I didn't want to compromise that. So I gave up my membership of Rethink, and resolved to stop trying to agitate for change. Change was of the time, I reminded myself. It was not my job to change the world.

But then one day, Rethink Mental Illness contacted me by phone. I was no longer a member of the charity, but they told me that they were organising a National Psychosis Summit and would like me to be a consultant. I was immediately flattered – a consultant. That sounded important. In the end, the work consisted of no more than a few phone calls and a day's attendance at the conference itself. But on that day I travelled to London for the first time in almost a year, and sat in the Church House Conference Centre in Westminster listening to the opening addresses, feeling as though I had somehow arrived. It was a beautiful building. The hall was large, wood-panelled, with a high domed roof. The roof was wooden and inscribed with Latin words. I felt that I mattered, that I was important purely by virtue of being there.

The event turned out to be a bit of a personal fiasco though. I had been over-keen to contribute in the various workshops as usual, but by the day's end, I took it a step further. In the summing up session, back in the grand circular hall, I put my hand up to have my say and was handed the microphone. I am not even sure what I said – almost certainly the same old stuff about diagnosis and recovery - but I do know that I said it for far too long, and much too repetitively. When the mic was finally wrenched from my clammy grip, I turned to my neighbour and pulled a face, which was intended to say, 'Oh dear, my tongue did run away with me,' but which actually announced, 'Look at me, I am totally bonkers!'

I was mortified. I realised that I had not disgraced myself by any objective standard, but I felt humiliated. I was tired and miserable and I just wanted to get home. Miserable and self-denigrating thoughts took hold. I was not well-equipped to speak with any degree of clarity or authority…I was useless…I was not contributing usefully to reform of the mental health system.

Once again, I vowed that this would be my last event, and this time I acted on it - the next day I called the Rethink Campaigns manager to inform her that I would no longer be participating in campaigns. She was very sweet and very concerned about what had led me to this decision and she tried to assure me that my contribution was valuable and so on. But I had had enough. After every single mental health event I had ever attended, I had felt the same – wrung out, over-exposed, full of self-doubt.

I knew that, objectively speaking, this was not the debacle it felt to me. I was not the first person to have suffered from verbal diarrhoea when in possession of a microphone and faced by a room full of people. But, for me, it was the final straw. From now on, I resolved, I would avoid speaking in public about mental health and instead I would stay home and write. I would write about breakdown and recovery, and I would put down every single thing I could think of on the subject. And then I would move on. I would maybe write romance, maybe in some other genre, but I would definitely stick to fiction and hopefully I would make it light.

I would keep up my blog. I would still try to communicate the messages I felt so strongly about – that mental health treatment should never be forced upon an individual, that the doom-laden word 'schizophrenia' stops people recovering. These things were so important to me. But I could attend another one hundred public events and re-iterate my views without making any noticeable difference to anyone and the personal cost to myself was too great.

Change would happen with or without me. I had to move on.

I kept a toe in the waters though. I had met a lady called Vanessa Pinfold through Rethink, when she had worked as research assistant to the Schizophrenia Commission. When she later left to set up her own charity she recruited people with experience of mental illness to work with her. In the summer of 2013 I had been invited to London, with other 'experts by experience' for an initial meeting at the McPin Foundation. The idea was to see whether working as peer researchers for McPin would suit us. I was paid for my attendance and had a good day there, meeting lots of like-minded people.

At the end of the day I had walked back to the train station with Terry Bowyer, the Commissioner I had met two years earlier, who had also been at the meeting. We sat together on the train and spoke at length about various aspects of 'schizophrenia' and about recovery from mental illness in particular. 'You have to write about recovery,' Terry told me. 'You are very unusual in that you have made a full recovery without medication. Other people need to know about it'. I had been planning this book anyway, but Terry's comment spurred me on.

Terry shared the same diagnosis as me. He was a very strong and articulate person who had built himself a successful life, but for whatever reason, he couldn't manage without psychiatric medication (although he had tried to do so several times). I resolved after our conversation that if I could ever get to the bottom of whatever it was that had enabled me to recover and use the information to help others to do the same, then I would.

I hoped that I would be chosen to work with the McPin Foundation, who seemed to be genuinely interested in pioneering and researching a new approach to the treatment of emotional distress. A short while later I was delighted to hear that I had indeed been successful, and in February 2014 I attended an induction day meeting. It was not long before I was asked to help with some research work for McPin and I have done several pieces of work for them in the time since. I feel that this work is useful and relevant to my interests and I am really proud to be involved with the organisation.

CHAPTER TWENTY-THREE
Book Reviews

The income for my memoir had dwindled over the years, but reviews were still coming in, slowly. They were mostly good, because most people are kind and don't review a book unless they like it. A few critical reviewers complained that there wasn't enough detail about the illness itself (this had been deliberate because I didn't want the book to make overly grim reading). Other reviewers said that I was definitely misdiagnosed, that it was not possible that I'd had schizophrenia and fully recovered.

I didn't respond – it's not professional to reply to reviewers – but I wrote about these subjects a lot in my blog. The fact is, I didn't really know whether I had ever had schizophrenia. I would certainly have liked to think that I never had it. What I did know though (and would never forget) was that I had been very ill indeed, quite out of control in fact. However, I had learned over recent years that emotional distress is very hard to categorise and indeed that categorising it is not helpful. I had enough symptoms to convince those observing my behaviour that I fitted into that dreadful-sounding category – Schizophrenic - but my prognosis certainly had not turned out to match the one I had been given.

And I was sure that if I did once have schizophrenia, I no longer had it. I was not perfect by any means – there were plenty of things that I would have liked to improve about myself. But my mental health was about average, I thought. I didn't hear voices and I didn't have hallucinations, and I didn't take any medication to stop these things happening. So, surely I could not, technically, be schizophrenic?

In fact, there was strong proof now that mental breakdowns could and should be short acute episodes, but that incorrect treatment, especially long-term use of anti-psychotics, turned them into chronic illnesses, and effectively disabled many people. Reading the work of Robert Whitaker and others on the subject, I felt extremely lucky to have escaped those drugs.

I welcomed the fact that people bothered to review my book. Even negative reviews provided useful feedback. I had written the memoir to show that anyone can suffer from mental illness - not to say 'I am fatally flawed' but to say, 'we are all flawed, but it doesn't have to matter' and most people who read it, I considered, had understood that message.

I did feel hurt when somebody commented on my blog that she/he had lost interest in it because I kept repeating myself. I realised it was fair comment though – I repeat myself a good deal in real life too! And, I reasoned, I could do so on my blog, if I wished. In fact, I probably will keep on repeating myself ad infinitum, until or unless the things I feel are important change. (I apologise in advance for the amount of repetition in this book).

The hardest thing was when people made personal comments – for example, one reviewer said that I was very self-centred. Again, this was probably correct in a way – after all, anyone who writes a memoir is writing about themselves. The way it was said was rather unkind though – and it is my nature (perhaps the nature of any writer) to take criticism to heart. I could read twenty lovely reviews of my book and be very happy and grateful for them, but it was the one nasty one that seemed to stick in my mind. The only solution, I knew, was to develop a tougher skin.

I was excited one day when I found my book on Goodreads, with lots of reviews that I had never seen before. I also sometimes received letters and emails from people who had read my book. And by now I felt that some of the people I had met through my blog were real friends. There was no doubt about it, my interest in mental health had enhanced my life. I was disillusioned with it in some ways, but I probably would never be ready to give it up entirely.

CHAPTER TWENTY-FOUR
The Diagnosis

My happiest times, as I have said, were when home life was at the forefront, and mental health issues took a back seat. At times like this it didn't seem to matter how some misguided psychiatrists had classified me, years and years previously. But sometimes the diagnosis seemed to hang heavily over me, casting its shadow on everything I tried to achieve and at those times I longed to be rid of it.

One day I read in a newspaper article that Sinead O'Connor had now realised that she was misdiagnosed with bipolar disorder. She had been reassessed by three independent psychiatrists who verified that she did not have the condition and she was now in the process of coming off her medications. I applauded her wholeheartedly and began to dream of trying to get my own diagnosis recanted.

Soon afterwards I went along to see 'Dr Jameson', the last psychiatrist who had treated me, after Amy was born. It wasn't easy to get an appointment, but I managed to persuade the GP to write me a referral. I wanted to ask the psychiatrist to either retract the diagnosis or to record my recovery from it. On one level I knew this wasn't likely to happen, because it would mean admitting that either a mistake had been made in the diagnosis or that schizophrenia was not a lifetime disease of the brain after all and either of these admissions would have had repercussions. But I thought that, faced with a person who was clearly capable of reasoning and functioning, with no psychiatric symptoms and who had not been on medication for many years, the doctor – a kind and capable man – would not be able to refute the fact that I had recovered.

In fact, Dr Jameson himself had suggested many years previously that the diagnosis was wrong, but had then changed his attitude after meeting with the rest of his 'team'. I just hoped that another ten years of remaining symptom-free and off medication might have changed his mind.

The doctor was nice. He always had been. But his views had become more entrenched in the time since I had first met him. We had a long conversation, during which he spoke of assaults from patients in hospital, and insisted that forced medication was a necessity. He did write down some of the things I told him about alternative views of mental illness and recovery, but essentially I was just sitting, under the force of his mesmerising gaze, listening. It was like being hypnotised.

By the time I left that room I felt saddened, because this man was clearly very powerful – and could be a strong force for good, as he had been with my own health all those years ago. Now, it seemed, he was just a force, standing up for the way things were, for the way they had always been, not admitting any possibility of change or improvement in the system. I had been lucky to get the best of him, perhaps, before he became hardened by his years of working within the system as it stood. If he had worked within a more therapeutic system perhaps his outlook might have been different.

A few weeks later I received a letter confirming that the diagnosis had been the right one, at the time (although he thought that now if I presented with those symptoms it would be seen differently). The letter seemed to be a masterpiece of doublespeak – the diagnosis was right at the time, but would be wrong now? And yet it should still stand? I wondered what that actually meant. The letter also said I should be watchful for the return of symptoms. Which of course I always had been, although sometimes that had stood in the way of recovery. Real recovery, I was starting to realise, meant accepting that I was well, regardless of what others thought. Trusting myself.

I remembered the father of a University friend. He was retired when I met him, but he had used to work for the United Nations and he told me that one day a man had come into his office begging for a certificate of sanity. He was told that no such thing existed, but he insisted that he just wanted someone to write a letter to say that he was sane. My friend's father said that none of his colleagues (it was the department of health and hygiene or some such, as I remember) were prepared to furnish the chap with such a letter, but he understood, he said, and he did so.

I had listened carefully to my friend's Dad's story, and was impressed with its illustration of his humanity. However, I said with certainty, nobody should need such proof of their sanity, since it didn't matter a whit what others thought of them. The knowledge of a person's sanity resided with that person themselves and that was enough. I remember so clearly how the old man shook his head at me, clearly believing that I had failed to understand the lesson. Only now, all these years later, I understood his point.

I knew that I was sane now, but part of me longed –
would always long - for official confirmation of that
fact. I still envied Sinead O'Connor and wished I could
see three different psychiatrists as she did, and be told
definitively that I was not schizophrenic. I consoled
myself with the thought that I might pay privately to do
that one day, if I failed to ever come to terms with it all.

Meanwhile, I told myself that my memoir, and other
books I would write in the future, were one way of
getting such confirmation. Schizophrenics were not
supposed to be able to see projects through – well, I had
written and published a successful book. I had received
a glowing review from Raymond Briggs. I could tell an
engaging, coherent tale – therefore, I was not mad.
People would read my story and understand what
happened to me, why I became ill, and they would know
that I am better now. There would be no doubt that I
was normal.

I hoped.

CHAPTER TWENTY-FIVE
Majorca

In April 2014, shortly after the National Psychosis
Summit, we went on holiday to Spain. It was two years
since our first family trip in an aeroplane, and it felt like
a real treat to fly again. It was also bliss to be able to
totally relax once we reached our hotel. The kids were
contented, mainly because there was food and drink
available all day every day – the holiday was all-
inclusive. The children played around the pool, eating,
drinking, reading or listening to music, and Paul and I
just flaked out on the deckchairs. In the evenings we
went to bed early – the hotel did not have a room big
enough for all of us, or any adjoining rooms, so Paul
stayed in one room with the boys and I was in another
with the girls.

After our return, we all felt refreshed. Finally, I seemed
to have got on track with my writing. As spring came, I
fell into a routine, and I began to write quite prolifically,
coming up with three novellas and a children's book.
None of these books were art, and I knew that really I
should have spent more time to make them funnier and
more interesting. But I was only aiming to work as fast
as I could, to produce light writing for entertainment.
Together, the novellas alone had added up to fifty
thousand words in length– no mean feat in the space of
just a couple of months, I felt.

So I was progressing. But then I got distracted.
Originally I had planned to write more novellas in my
series, and then perhaps to join them into one full-length
novel. But I had never really put my heart into that
project and now I had pretty much lost interest in it.

Meanwhile, I had begun to research how to make money from writing, and I had discovered that romance sells better than anything else, and that out of all the sub-genres of romance, erotic fiction was currently selling the best (Fifty Shades of Grey had set this trend). So I decided that I would write to this formula. I would produce erotic romance. It didn't have to be art (and it was extremely unlikely to be) but it would make enough money for that not to matter. In time, when I had produced enough trash and made enough money, I could get back to 'proper' writing.

So I told myself. And I promptly wrote reams of rubbish, page upon page, thousands of words of it. If Paul or the children came in while I was writing, I would hurriedly shut off the computer. I made Paul promise that when he was uploading my book to publish on Amazon Kindle, he would not read it. If he did, I told him, I would never write erotic fiction again. However, it really wasn't doing me any good. I felt so ashamed of what I was writing, so embarrassed in case one day somebody would find out that it was my work. I started to feel that it was worse than rubbish, i.e. it was so badly written that nobody want to read it and it would not make a penny. And I also began to worry that perhaps I would never be able to write anything of quality again, if I let myself descend to this level.

And yet I ploughed on. I had to finish the book, I told myself. It wouldn't matter if I never wrote another one, but now I was twenty thousand words through and I couldn't waste all the time I had spent on it. However, I was increasingly losing heart in my work. I tried to reason with myself about it – after all, my book wasn't nearly as saucy as Fifty Shades. It was almost

93

respectable in comparison. But writing it made me feel dirty.

Then I had another brainwave. Instead of giving up on my book, I would improve it, I told myself. I would give it more of a story, take out the rudest bits. Make it something I could live with having written, even if it would never be something I was proud of. So I took out the rude bits. But then I realised that there really wasn't much of a book without them, and so I put them back in again and carried on writing.

I went on like this for several weeks, starting and stopping, until one morning I sat down to work and ended up deleting all of the thirty thousand words that I had written so far. I texted Paul at work to tell him what I had done, worried that he might be annoyed about all the time I had wasted, but he texted back immediately to say that he thought it was the right decision. He could see how tormented I had been by the whole business. Even if I never made a penny from writing, he said, it didn't matter. I knew I was lucky that Paul was so supportive, and I resolved to make him proud of me. I would write more books, but from now on I would write them from my heart.

CHAPTER TWENTY-SIX
A Day at Roedean

The internet was wonderful, I thought, for bringing old friends together. I had contacted various school friends through Facebook over the years, and now through Twitter I found another old friend. This girl (or woman, now, I supposed) Sasha, was from Roedean, where I had spent three years between the ages of about ten and thirteen. Sasha had read my book and contacted me to say that she was very impressed with it. She told me that she had spoken to the editor of the old school magazine, and that they would be delighted if I would write a piece about my book for them.

I had always been very nostalgic about Roedean. The years I had spent there had been some of the happiest of my life, and I cherished the memories. However, I felt that my life had diverged so far from the usual route that I had very little in common with my old school friends these days. In fact, I was worried that if I ever met any of them in real life they would find me contemptible - although my communications with Sasha via the internet had put my mind at rest on this count, to some extent.

Anyhow, we had booked a short break in the early summer, in a youth hostel on the South Downs. It was close to Roedean, so the evening before we left I looked up the old school website, to see if it would be possible to visit with Paul and the children. To my amazement, the day we were travelling to the area, the 21st June, was Open Day at Roedean. I phoned the school and was told that we would be welcome to join in. I then contacted Sasha through Twitter, who said that she would be there and was really excited about the prospect of meeting again.

So we made our way to Roedean, arriving in the middle of the morning. I had been concerned that our family might look and feel out of place, but in fact the experience turned out to be oddly therapeutic. Sasha was as lovely as I remembered, and she introduced me to another girl, Sara, who had used to be in my class. Paul and I chatted with them, as the girls listened and the boys made constant forages to the table in the marquee to load their plates up with more cream cakes.

Both Sasha and Sara praised my book and told the children that they should all be very proud of me for writing it. Anna had pretty much got over her embarrassment about the book anyway by that point, but I think that encounter helped to banish the last vestige of any shame she felt about me and I will always be really grateful to my old school friends for that.

We were just one of a number of visiting families, and perhaps we had different backgrounds and means to some of the others, but I came away from Roedean that afternoon feeling as though I really was a part of the old school. I also felt validated. I had a reinforced sense of certainty that, although people may have vastly different paths through life, none of us are no more or less worthy as a result.

It was all to do with how you perceived yourself, I realised. The main advantage of these prestigious private schools was that they managed to endow their pupils with confidence, and this confidence was invaluable in helping them to thrive despite any difficulties they encountered later. Although I had only spent a few years at Roedean, they were formative years and I wondered now whether the influence of that school had perhaps been a factor in my recovery.

We slept at the hostel (youth hostels all have private rooms available now, which sleep up to six people, which is perfect for a family of our size. Whenever we stay in a hotel, Paul and I have to sleep in separate rooms with two children each, so although it felt odd to be sleeping in bunk beds and the hostel accommodation left a lot to be desired in other respects, it was good to be all together). The next day we headed up to Brighton and drifted about there, for a while, had lunch and then drove home. When we got back, I wrote my piece for the Old Roedeanian magazine and sent it off. I was really looking forward to seeing it in print.

CHAPTER TWENTY-SEVEN
Everyone Judges a Book by its Cover

To my surprise, while we were in Spain, sales of my memoir had leapt. Up to that point they had been seriously flagging, as was only to be expected from a book that had already been out for three years. But I had recently done a promotion on Amazon Kindle, and although these promotions had not had much of an effect on sales for some time, for some reason this one really did.

I was really pleased that the book was earning some money again, and I started to devote a good deal of time to promoting my work on Facebook and Twitter. Throughout the rest of April, and May, I networked online, and I was rewarded by high book sales in May too. I had been encouraged too, recently, by the thriving and supportive mental health recovery community on Twitter, which had given me the sense that progress was being made in the world, that mental health was gradually being de-stigmatized.

I decided to use some of the unexpected new earnings to republish my book, using a professional cover designer. I sent an email to Raymond Briggs, asking if he would mind me using his kind quotes about my book on my new front cover. I was not really expecting to hear back from him, but to my delight I did, the very next day – and he said it was fine to use his quotes! I was proud all over again when I saw his wonderful words printed on the front of my book.

I was so excited to see if the new cover would have a positive effect on sales – and delighted when it did. I kept up with Twitter after that. It was important to keep a balance between writing and promoting books, of course, and it didn't take me long to realise that marketing could suck up a great deal of time. Promotion served a dual purpose, though, providing an opportunity to connect with others online, and I enjoyed it for that reason.

CHAPTER TWENTY-EIGHT
Summer 2014

The last weeks before the end of term were always incredibly busy, and so as usual I was glad when the school holidays began. The weather turned out to be glorious and we spent a lot of time at the beach (sharing a beach hut with other families had become a firm habit over the past few years). Over the course of the summer I made up my mind to stop running the writing group at the library. I had dithered over the decision for a while, but in the end I decided that it was more important to concentrate on my own writing and not get side-tracked.

Attendance at the group had gradually fallen in any case, and there were plenty of other local writing groups that people could join if they wished. So my time (or at least Monday to Friday in term time and during school hours) was completely clear for writing. Then I backtracked a little, by agreeing to work with Anton again. He was bored and demotivated now that his autobiography was finally finished and published, so I arranged to give him private writing lessons for an hour each week. He really enjoyed the lessons and was always full of ideas for new writing projects. I felt that I was doing him a good turn (he paid me, which helped of course) but I resolved not to undertake any other commitments.

CHAPTER TWENTY-NINE
The End (I hope)

In October 2014, I was approached by the Huffington Post (an online newspaper with a worldwide readership of one hundred million people!) who asked me to blog for them on the subject of mental health. My first blog post, on the theme of Living with Schizophrenia, was published on World Mental Health Day.

I wrote another post shortly afterwards, about anxiety, and another about pet therapy, and then I stalled. I felt over-exposed. I started to doubt whether it was worth writing and publishing books at all. I faffed about and chased my tail for a bit. And then I knuckled down again, got on with things, and settled down and finished this book...

So, that brings me right up to the current moment. I consider myself to be healed of mental illness – which is not to say that I think I am perfect in any way. The most interesting thing about my recovery, I think, is that it only really took place when I recognised that it was already a reality. I had been well for some time before it even struck me that I was better because I had been so effectively brainwashed into believing that this was an impossibility.

Once I refused to accept other people's opinions of me any longer and instead took a look at the reality of my own life, I realised that I am just the same as anyone else I know. I am not a schizophrenic. Nor are you, and nor is any person you know. We are all human beings and as long as we live peacefully and try to be good people we should be free from the interference or judgement of others. I honestly do not think that any person should have the power to label another schizophrenic, knowing as I do of the permanent damage that this diagnosis inflicts.

So, I am probably about as well as I am ever going to be. I am, as I mentioned, a bit worried about the reception of this book, which I fear that readers may find rather dull in comparison to my first memoir. However, I have done my best with it and I really hope that it will inspire and motivate others in their personal recoveries. I think that perhaps we are all on a permanent spectrum of health, both mental and physical – maybe nobody is ever entirely well – but most of the time, I am pretty happy with my life as it is. Which is, I think, about as much as anyone on this planet can wish for and certainly more than I ever would have expected in my younger days.

PART TWO

ON LIVING

After I gave an author talk at Newcastle University, back in 2012, a student asked me, 'What would have helped?' She went on, 'Obviously, nothing helped you at the time, until you decided to help yourself. But what could have been done differently, what action from mental health professionals do you consider would have been beneficial to your recovery?' It seemed to me to be a very pertinent question, and it was one that kept coming back to me in subsequent years.

To answer it, I needed to cast my mind back over the fourteen or so years since my last (and final) breakdown. So here are my answers to that question, in no particular order. Some of this will repeat the story I have told in the previous section – this is intentional, in case any readers wished to skip that part of the book and move on to this section instead.

I have been in the process of writing this recovery book for several years, and I kept dithering about the form of it. At one point I was going to write it as a kind of textbook, but I worried that it would be too dry. So I decided to return to the tried and tested memoir format – but then I was concerned that would be rather a long and tedious read which would not make the message about recovery clear enough.

Then I stumbled across a book by Stephen King, 'On Writing'. I loved this book. The first part was about his life, or 'How one writer was formed,' and the second part was about the craft of writing itself. The beauty of self-publishing, of course, is that you can write however you want, but 'On Writing' is my excuse for never quite making up my mind about the style of this one, which has turned out to be part memoir, part recovery manual. I have paraphrased King's title as the heading for this part of the book. (I stole the title of my first book too, from E Fuller Torrey's Surviving Schizophrenia. That was for the opposite reason – not because I admire his book, but because I despise it. There is more about that below).

A Caveat (A long time ago, I studied some Latin at school, and still like to utilise the occasional term. Also, caveat has much more of a ring to it than 'Warning').

So here's the caveat: I am not the Oracle (I did actually believe once that I was the Oracle, but at that time I was held in hospital under a section of the Mental Health Act). But I have suffered extreme emotional distress, had several severe breakdowns and recovered from them, and I feel the need to share the nuts and bolts of my recovery, in the hope that I may point the way forward to others who find themselves in a similar position.

I am well aware that what has worked for me might not work for others; my experiences may not be applicable to their situations at all. I still want to try to help. So please, read on, but be aware that I am not an expert on the mental health of other people. I don't believe anyone really is – we are all privy only to the secrets of our own minds and can only ever be experts on our own mental health.

I was very mentally ill indeed, on three occasions. The

last time I had a breakdown was more than fourteen years ago, and now I have recovered to the point where I am settled and happy with my life. (Married life and four children might send some people who don't even have a history of nerves completely up the wall, but for me it is a dream come true). I strongly feel there is a need for practical advice for those who suffer nervous breakdowns/emotional distress/psychosis.

A lot of people recover from serious mental illness, but they often do not share the details of their recovery. Understandably, they brush their past history under the carpet, because they are concerned that if people found out about it, they would be stigmatised (and they are right; they would be). I know full recovery is possible, even for those people who, like me, have a diagnosis of schizophrenia, and I want to explain exactly how I achieved it.

For a long time I thought it was not even possible to give this sort of advice. People are so individual that there is no definitive answer to emotional distress. For example, looking back at my own situation, I think I might have benefitted from being more open about my problems and worries – but then, some others who are very open seem to become dependent on the help they are given and then find it difficult to operate independently in the future.

I have particular views – for example, I am rather obsessed with the unhelpfulness of diagnosis. A lot of other people do not mind their diagnosis at all, and do find it helpful. They may also see the psychiatric medication they are given as a necessity – this is, of course, well within their rights. I, on the other hand, resent being labelled 'schizophrenic'. I also take pride in being medication-free. (I think on some level this is because I feel it proves that the psychiatrists were wrong, because they said I could never manage without it. Mostly it is just because I hate the way being on medication feels).

I do not advocate that my way is the only way, or the right way to recovery. This is just what has worked for me, so far, and for some reason I feel the need to share my experiences with the world. Psychiatrists would probably refer to this as a delusion of grandeur – and they might well be right. But I still hope that my advice may help someone else who has suffered, or is suffering, emotional distress to find a way through, to begin to believe in themselves again.

WHAT WOULD HAVE HELPED?
1. WRITING

In the first part of this book I mentioned my first memoir, published just over three years ago, 'Surviving Schizophrenia'. I wrote the book in my maiden name, Louise Gillett. I have young children, and my married name is very distinctive – therefore although I had no intention of hiding my identity (my photo was on the front cover of the original edition and is still on the back cover of the paperback!) I felt that it would be a sensible precaution to use a pen name, so as not to draw too much attention to myself at the outset. Admitting publicly to a diagnosis of schizophrenia seemed like an act of madness in itself when I first published the book, and I wanted to mitigate any possible harm to myself or my family.

I first wrote my story in the form of a blog. I started the blog in 2009, and I called it, 'Schizophrenia at the Schoolgate'. This is where I honed my writing skills – I wrote the blog for eighteen months, almost on a daily basis. I started writing anonymously – my worst fear then was that my diagnosis would become public knowledge. But then the blog itself began to surprise me, as it evolved from a simple recounting of my story to an investigation of mental illness itself.

I discovered other blogs on the subject, and began to realise that there was more to the subject of schizophrenia than I had ever realised. I found out that the diagnosis of schizophrenia that I had been given as a nineteen year old girl – a label which basically said that I was, and always would be, a lunatic – a label which I had accepted because I trusted the medical profession –

was based on completely spurious science.

I discovered writers like Robert Whitaker and Richard Bentall. I found websites such as 'Mad in America'. And I began to realise, slowly, that 'schizophrenia' was not a genetic condition, or a brain disease. That anyone, given enough stress, could suffer a nervous breakdown, as I had done. That those who suffered such breakdowns in third world countries, where there was less access to psychiatric medication, fared much better, recovering completely in much greater numbers than we do in the UK and the USA.

As I began to realise how nebulous a diagnosis of schizophrenia is, my fear of this so-called 'brain disease' began to lessen. The more I learned, the more courage I took from what I had discovered, and after a while I stopped writing anonymously, and made the blog public.

My story just seemed to be demanding to be written, and in the end I gave in to it, and decided to publish my autobiography after all. I thought that when it was done I could put all that behind me and get on with the task of writing fiction. I had the story already, written over years. But I knew it needed organising and tidying up. To give myself time and space to do this, I attended a short writing course at the Arvon Foundation in Devon where I received encouragement and motivation and when I returned from that course I spent the best part of a year updating the book, and then self-published it on Amazon Kindle.

I chose the title because there is another work of the same name, 'Surviving Schizophrenia,' written by a chap called E. Fuller Torrey. This book was written many years ago, but has been re-issued in various editions since. Fuller Torrey does not agree that there is a hereditary element to schizophrenia (it was interesting for me to learn that his sister was diagnosed with the disease). Apart from that though, the book perpetuates all the myths of schizophrenia – that it is a disease of the brain, completely incurable, but that sufferers can be helped to achieve a better quality of life. All myths that have been completely disproved by writers like Robert Whitaker, but that somehow endure anyway. Fuller Torrey is also an avid supporter of forced medication and incarceration for those suffering from serious mental illness, which I find disturbing. By appropriating the name of the book I thought that I might deflect some of the people searching for it, to my own work, where they would then get an alternative view of the matter.

Writing my memoir helped me immeasurably. I wrote it for altruistic reasons; because I wanted to help others (admittedly this desire to help was prompted by guilt that I had recovered from my experience of mental illness and so many others had not). I loved the wonderful feedback I received, which confirmed to my delight that I had in fact been of help to many people – but what surprised me was that the person who received the most benefit from all of this was me.

I felt liberated by opening up after so many years of hiding my diagnosis. I realised that the people who mattered the most to me would always support me, and that anybody who thought less of me because of what I divulged in my memoir was not really of any relevance or importance in my life. Anyway, there were surprisingly few people who had a negative outlook and many who just seemed quite neutral – life went on just as it had always done, except that I felt an overwhelming sense of relief.

The most important and life-changing effect of writing my book was that, by the time I finished, I found I was no longer afraid of the diagnosis I had been given, and I no longer believed in it. I had been designated 'Schizophrenic' by medical professionals who had observed my behaviour and thought it fitted a set of diagnostic criteria that justified bestowing this label on me. They thought that somehow this would help me – that I would benefit from accepting the 'fact' that I had a 'brain disease' and taking drugs to treat it for the rest of my life.

There is no objective test for schizophrenia – no brain scan or blood test to prove its existence or absence. However, I respected mental health professionals, and was willing to accept that they knew something about me that I did not. It was only many years later, when my life did not turn out to fit the prognosis that I had been given – when I did not deteriorate mentally, when I managed to exist without medication, that I began to suspect that perhaps somebody might have got it wrong. By that time, I had learned a lot more about mental health than I had originally known – which I will expand on in the next section of this book, on reading and education.

I always felt that I was a writer – even before I had properly set pen to paper and so had no actual evidence for this belief. Sometimes I wondered if it was an irrational belief – a delusion of grandeur. My memoir however, sold many more copies than I had dared to hope, and began to provide me with a small income.

Within a year I was able to give up disability benefits, the crutch that had sustained me throughout the long period of my recovery. My confidence and self-esteem grew as a result. I was so pleased to be contributing to the family finances through my own efforts. I was proudest of all to be able to say out loud, at last, that I was a writer!

But this part of the book is not supposed to be about me. Writing is, I believe, my vocation, but I firmly believe that writing has therapeutic benefits for everybody. Starting from writing 'To do' lists in an attempt to be more organised, progressing to emails and letters to keep in touch, and to diary writing to offload the day's worries, continuing all the way to blogging, poetry, life writing or creating a new world within the pages of a short story or novel – all of it is a valuable way of documenting or sharing the human experience.

So that is my first tip for becoming and remaining mentally well – write! You will be surprised at what a valuable tool it will become for your recovery. Write a diary, to begin with, or a series of random notes on things that you are thinking about or that have been worrying you. Write anything at all. And then, if you can, formulate these thoughts into short poems, or longer ones. Make them into stories. Our story-telling ability is vital to us as humans. If we can put our thoughts and feelings into words, if we can communicate them, this goes a long way to keeping us well.

Certain writing exercises can be particularly useful, when they help us to think in positive ways. For example, when I am feeling down, I find that my thinking becomes negative, and this negativity can quickly set in and start to become a habit. So I regularly write a short piece – a page or two – with the title, 'Things I am looking forward to'. There is always something to look forward to – the children singing at their Christmas concerts, a family outing to the beach, or a birthday. And I find that my outlook is much more cheerful once I have made myself concentrate on these things for a few minutes, by writing about them. Try it and see!

(I still write my blog, incidentally, but I fear that it is not the useful resource it once was. For example, around the time of my bunion operation it was peppered with references to antibiotics and stitches, and sometimes I write about my children – not often, but sometimes. I want them to grow up to be understanding and caring individuals and I do not think they should ever be ashamed of having a mother who once had mental health problems. I want them to be aware of the fact that they are not tainted by association with me – although I know that all teenagers will be embarrassed of their parents at some point in time. But all this personal stuff certainly detracts from the usefulness of my blog as a mental health resource.

WHAT WOULD HAVE HELPED?
2. READING

Once, a few years after my second breakdown, I started
to have disturbing thoughts. These seemed to happen
out of the blue, when I first woke in the morning and
before I went to sleep at night. The most frequent
thought, and the one that bothered me most, was, 'I want
to die'. It scared me. I had never been suicidal, or not
knowingly, but perhaps, I thought, my unconscious was
now trying to give me a message. Otherwise, at that
time, I had no symptoms of mental ill health. I went to
the GP about another matter, and for some reason, at the
end of the session when he asked if there was anything
else bothering me, I confided in him about the thoughts.
He smiled, and at first I thought he was laughing at me.

But he was not – he was smiling in sympathy, and he
went on to tell me about hypnopompic and hypnagogic
thoughts, which basically are odd ideas that can
randomly enter the mind just before falling asleep or just
prior to waking. He was a young man, probably not long
out of medical school, and I think I was very lucky to see
him that day – I am not sure that an older GP would not
have known about this or bothered to communicate it to
me. I was really grateful for the information and to my
amazement, as soon as I knew what I was suffering
from, the symptoms disappeared. The mind works in
some very peculiar ways.

Education confers power. Nowadays, all sorts of health
information and advice is readily available on the
internet and we can educate ourselves in the comfort of
our own homes. If you want to be a writer, you need to
read but even if you never write, and never want to, you

should read anyway. It shouldn't be a trial or a chore –
there are so many brilliant books out there, of all
different sorts, that are really, properly life-enhancing,
and informative too.

When I was really ill, in hospital at the age of nineteen, I
lost the ability to read. The words seemed to separate out
into letters and they no longer made sense. I found this
really alarming, especially because I had been able to
read since before I formed memories. I hated it. I was
determined not to give in though. I read anything –
starting with children's books – until the ability to
decipher their meaning returned properly, and I was so
happy when it did. And now I read for hours every day.

I stopped reading for a while after I had my children, but
am so glad that I joined a book group which encouraged
me to begin to read for pleasure again. I think it must
have helped my brain start to function again – it
certainly helped my concentration. As for what to read –
anything will do. Magazines, newspapers, blogs, self-
help books. Novels. There is so much to know, so much
to wonder over, in the printed word.

Read. Please. You will learn so much. It will help you
heal. You can join a book group, online or in the real
world, with a group of friends or at your local library,
because reading can be a social enterprise too and
anything which gets you out mixing with other people is
good.

Reading will make you realise that the human race
encompasses a huge array of variety in outlook and
behaviour but that we are all normal, in our own unique
ways. And it will introduce you to new, better, more

fascinating books.

Personally, I love self-help books, although I always resolve to do the exercises in them more slowly and thoroughly and I never do, so I suppose I do not reap their full benefit. But here is a short list of those sort of books that I feel have helped me: Selfhood by Dr Terry Lynch, Overcoming Low Self-Esteem by Melanie Ferrell, various books on CBT, A Sane New World by Ruby Wax (it always helps to read about a celebrity suffering emotional troubles, it reminds us that we are all in the same boat. It's even better when they find a way through their suffering, and show us the way by example).

These are just a few books, literally summoned up off the top of my head. There are many more useful books out there. I would advise that you should learn as much as possible on the subject of mental health and you don't even need books for this - there are various brilliant blogs too. The one that springs to mind is the Mad in America site - which is packed with information, containing many stories of people who have found their way through their experiences of emotional distress and who have even become stronger as a result of them.

When I went to the Schizophrenia Commission meeting in London in April 2102, I was very impressed with one of the other 'Delegates'. He was Asian, clearly a hard-working and upstanding person with a very good attitude towards his condition. He said he had taken the breakdown as an opportunity to improve himself, to study, and had taken all the courses he could manage while he was unwell. He had approached his situation – despite the awful diagnosis – as an opportunity to improve himself. And he had got well as a result.

As far as education about mental health goes, my aim would be that everyone knows what psychosis is, what can trigger it, and how to recover from it. When I was nineteen I opened a Sunday newspaper to read it, and thought all the news stories were about me. I turned on the television and thought the presenter of the programme was addressing me alone. I was terrified by the chaotic sense of the world spinning and fragmenting about me, and I had literally no idea what was happening.

I really hope that a nineteen year old in the future who experiences such things will be able to think, 'Ah, so this is psychosis,' and will know exactly where to turn to for help. Education about mental health is just as important as that about physical health – it should be a fundamental human right to know about and understand these things. And then, there would be no more distress and no more tragedy. Any person who heard a voice would immediately recognise this as a symptom of mental ill health and could trust in the mental health system to help, without fear of unpleasant repercussions.

WHAT WOULD HAVE HELPED?
3. SELF CARE

It is really hard to live a healthy life, and I know this from personal experience. But it is a fact that body and mind are indistinguishable – to have complete health in one the other must be healthy too. And to be in optimum health we have to learn to live without props like alcohol and cigarettes.

I don't say this flippantly – I understand that it's hard to stop smoking. I know that many people find it hard to manage without alcohol. I realise that even suggesting such things would be beneficial is contentious in itself. However, I know that it is possible to learn to function without these props and I believe that for people with experience of mental illness (extreme emotional distress) it is important to do so, in order to give oneself the best possible chance of recovery.

Further, if we can give our bodies only the best food, and the right amount of it, we will be healthier in body and mind. We must get our bodies in shape in order to give our minds the optimum chance of functioning well.

Another, similar point - sleep is a great healer. (Although you can sleep too much, which is bad for your health – eight hours a night is about right for most people).

Sorry if I am merely stating the obvious here, but I am going to persevere. We need exercise too – our bodies need to walk, to run, to swim. Our minds benefit from exercise too. When we get our bodies in order, our minds will have a much better chance of following suit.

I am in danger of being repetitive, and I am sure you get my point by now. Mind and body are linked, you need to get your body in shape so that your mind can function properly. There, I have repeated it again. Sorry, but I cannot overemphasise the importance of this.

It may take some time, but start now. Work on your body, increase your physical fitness, do the best you can to give yourself a fighting chance of health and happiness. Take it slowly, and take the time to appreciate what you are doing for yourself.

It's not easy. But I managed these things and so I know that you can too.

You may sometimes fall short of your ideals, but please keep trying to be the best that you can be, physically. I still fall short myself – I followed a gluten free diet for quite a while and found that it suited me, but I slipped back into eating grains again some time ago. I do exercise daily – luckily for me I have dogs that insist on being walked – and I try to eat as healthily as I can manage. I am always trying to improve these things. And I am only offering the advice that I think will help, unpopular though it might be. I am not saying that you cannot be mentally healthy unless you are physically healthy. I am just suggesting that improving the condition of your body is something that is within your power to achieve, and that if you make the effort (which does sometimes seem like a superhuman effort) to do so, you will undoubtedly feel the benefit on your journey to recovery.

For more practical advice, please look at Monica

Cassini's blog, Beyond Meds. Despite the title, this blog is not all about stopping medication – (although it does acknowledge the fact that this is possible for some people under some circumstances). It has a lot of advice about healthy living and eating. I didn't use it in my recovery, because I only discovered it relatively recently, but I am sure that it is an invaluable resource for many people.

WHAT WOULD HAVE HELPED?
4. GETTING BUSY

A fundamental part of my recovery came from keeping myself busy. Without something to do, I would have spent hours thinking, brooding over my worries and problems, which would not have helped to solve them in any way.

Once I started having children, I was constantly occupied, and I never looked back. The time around Anna's birth was truly awful – I was intensely deluded. I remember in the maternity hospital (where Anna was in special care) drawing diagrams which somehow, to me, explained every conundrum I could think of. The diagrams were a plan of Anna's future.

I remember Paul trying to humour me, although on some level I sensed that he was upset and confused by my behaviour. I was very paranoid. I was suspicious of the nursing staff and of everyone else I came into contact with. Before long I was sectioned and I spent three months in hospital – the most frightening time in my life. But it passed, and I went home with our baby.

Every morning since I had Anna, I had a reason to get out of bed. And as my baby grew up, I made sure to lead an exceedingly calm and ordered life. I read a lot about bringing up children and I knew that they needed security, routine, guidelines, structured activities and so on. I set about creating the best environment I could for my child.

I walked her constantly in her pram. I joined mother and toddler groups, where at first I was hampered by my nerves. Conversation had always seemed something of a mystery to me. My mother was not a communicator, to the extent that she would often not even dignify my attempts at talking to her with a reply, so I had an inferiority complex from very early on when it came to judging whether or not I was interesting to others.

I had always listened carefully to others talking, but still had never been able to emulate them. So much of what people said seemed to be superfluous and pointless, yet they seemed to say it with such confidence and ease. It was a total puzzle as far as I was concerned.

Now, however, I had a subject to talk about – babies. I was becoming increasingly knowledgeable on that subject, which other mothers seemed as happy as I was to converse about for hours. And these other mothers didn't seem to notice my personal defects, which diminished as a consequence. They talked about such simple subjects – nappies, baby milk and so on, that I found it quite easy to respond in kind. I was developing a satisfactory social life, almost without trying. I was quite satisfied with our little excursions, to baby groups and so on. Anna made friends, and their mothers became my friends too. It was quite a revelation.

Once Amy came along, then Scott and Luke, I literally had kids piling on my bed every morning, wanting attention. There was no option of not looking after them. I had to get up and get on with the day, however tired or incapable I felt. I was lucky that I was able to stay at home and look after my children until they all went to school. The process took twelve years. It was a long, calm interlude in my life, and in the process I became (I believe) quite well.

Motherhood was my path to recovery. Parenting, in my opinion, is a very healing experience. Through parenthood, you learn to love and to be loved. You learn to be patient, tolerant and calm. You finally begin to understand your own parents and the mistakes they made. You realise that no-one is perfect, but you have to keep on trying your best for the sake of your children.

However, although having a young family kept me busy – and happy - I do realise that many people find the converse – that having small children is an incredibly stressful time. It can cause mental health problems in people who have never had them previously, and exacerbate them in others.

Motherhood, domesticity, might not be your ambition, or might not be within your reach just now. So do anything. Any activity is a good thing. If you are worried about losing entitlement to benefits, which might be hard to recover if work proves to be beyond your capabilities at this time, then take on some voluntary work. Go for long walks – preferably with a friend for company. Keep yourself as busy as possible, so that you don't have time to think, or to be anxious. Let your brain have a break while your body takes over the work of recovery for a while.

If a friend or relative of mine ever has a mental breakdown, I will encourage them to think about it as an experience that has the potential to improve their lives. Psychosis can be a positive thing – it is the mind's way of showing that there is something seriously wrong with the direction of a person's life. If that person, after recovering from the psychosis, takes the right steps to change that direction, and if he or she can summon their strength to deal with any difficulties stemming from the breakdown itself, there is no reason why their life should not move forward. It took me a long time to learn that lesson, but I am keen to ensure that other young people should recover their equilibrium far more quickly than I did.

WHAT WOULD HAVE HELPED?
5. REJECTING THE DIAGNOSIS

I had six years in between my first and second breakdowns, before I was told that I had schizophrenia. During those years, I went about my business and my ignorance was bliss. I am pretty sure that I could not have coped with being told that I was schizophrenic when I was nineteen.

When I was told the diagnosis at the age of twenty-five, I accepted it as the truth. Now though, I am sure that it does not apply to me. I am no more a schizophrenic than I have ever been, despite what so-called experts might think. I do not need that label and when I believed that it applied to me it limited my life in many ways.

I am very aware of my mental health and if I feel uneasy, restless or stressed, I ask myself why, assess what it is that is making me feel this way, and take steps to remedy the situation. If I feel agitated, I make sure I calm myself. I am the person who knows my own mind best – in fact I am really the only person who knows it at all, and the same applies to every other human being in this world. So I am not going to give anyone else the power to inflict their understanding of me onto my life, ever again.

It is an interesting fact that the outcome for those people diagnosed bi-polar is far better than for those in receipt of a diagnosis of schizophrenia. This happens despite the fact that the symptoms are so similar that a lot of patients oscillate between one diagnosis and the other, and the medications are often exactly the same. Bi-polar disorder, like schizophrenia, is supposed to be a condition that necessitates medication for life.

The difference in outcomes can only be put down to the attitude of the 'patient' or sufferer. The fact is that a diagnosis of bi-polar disorder puts one in the same camp as Stephen Fry and Catherine Zeta-Jones as well as many high-functioning academics and professionals, whereas a diagnosis of schizophrenia puts one firmly in the camp of – unfortunately - the mad. This is, of course, only the case in the public perception of the illnesses, but each individual who suffers from mental illness is affected by these perceptions, and many of them learn to hold the same views themselves.

There is a body of opinion which says that so-called mental illness would be better considered as straightforward emotional distress. Many people – some of them qualified doctors or psychologists - who have had breakdowns themselves in the past and been labelled schizophrenic (Pat Deegan, Will Hall and Rufus May come to mind) feel that the medicalization of mental illness, the emphasis on forced treatment and on labelling (diagnosing) patients is completely wrong.

Psychiatrists, on the other hand, usually consider the symptoms of mental illness to be a manifestation of the problems of a diseased brain, not a malfunctioning mind, and insist that it is best treated by drugs. Although some practitioners of psychiatry acknowledge that problems in the course of a person's life may well have contributed to their breakdown, and will agree that the patient should have access to some kind of talking therapy as well as drugs, the basic stance of psychiatry is the medical model.

Schizophrenia, bi-polar and other related disorders are often compared to diabetes. Just as insulin is necessary for the diabetic so, it is said, anti-psychotic drugs are the only thing that will allow a schizophrenic or bi-polar patient to function – the view is that they do not cure the 'disease', they make it manageable. The reality, sadly, is that many people suffer further breakdowns while on these medications (as well as suffering extremely adverse, life-shortening, side-effects from the drugs).

Of course, my case proves that a so-called schizophrenic does not have to be on a lifelong regime of drugs. While I was writing this book, I consulted 'my' psychiatrist (the one I saw after the birth of each of my children) to ask whether I could now be considered to have recovered from schizophrenia. His conclusion was that I could not have recovered, because a person never recovers from this 'disease'. He also said (and confirmed in writing) that the diagnosis of schizophrenia is the correct one for my case, as confirmed by my medical notes that he had dug out and read over. The fact that I have led my life for the past fourteen years without any psychiatric medication and with no symptoms of psychosis – no voices, no delusions or hallucinations - was therefore officially irrelevant. The letter concluded by warning me that it would be prudent to keep watchful for any further signs of psychotic breakdown, as I will always be susceptible.

Is it just me, or does none of the above really make any sense? Are psychiatrists simply working in the dark – are the meanderings of the mind no clearer to them than to any of the rest of us? Unfortunately this is true – psychiatrists are operating on a system of guesswork. There is no brain scan to determine the presence or absence of mental illness, and the medication is largely ineffective. The psychiatrists are acting – almost always with the best of intentions, they are medical professionals after all – in accordance with what they think and hope will help the patient, while having no idea whether or not the medications they prescribe will have the result they are hoping for.

I don't think that psychiatrists make a diagnosis of schizophrenia with any intention of malice. I think they really believe that this is a medical condition, unfortunately an incurable one, and that their patients would do well to understand and accept this fact, and to operate within its limitations.

I do believe that this is misguided though. There is so much evidence to the contrary. And the good news is, plenty of people can and do recover. I am not the only one to have done so. Most people, once they are better, stay quiet about the diagnosis – as I did for many years. But about thirty per cent of people in the UK recover from serious mental illness – despite the burdens of the diagnosis and the medication – and by contrast about seventy per cent recover in undeveloped countries, where they are assimilated back into society and medication is not so readily available. (See the work of the notable writer Robert Whitaker). In Northern Finland, where the initial treatment for psychosis is not drugs but talking therapy – administered not in hospitals but in the patient's own home – the recovery rate is over ninety per cent.

I am not anti-medication. I just personally prefer not to take psychiatric drugs. I live a very clean life these days – I don't take drugs of any kind, I don't drink or smoke, I pay great attention to my diet and my sleep pattern. I am aware that such a puritanical way of life would not work for everyone (although I must say, I do still have fun, however it may sound!) I think that for someone who has suffered from serious mental illness in the past, such a way of life is helpful, but I am aware that some people get through life in other ways, and that one size does not fit all.

If medication is effective, then of course people should take it. However, it is a great pity that psychiatric medication does not work better and has so many damaging side-effects. In fact, in his book Anatomy of an Epidemic, Robert Whitaker shows how psychiatric medication actually worsens the outlook of those with mental illness. As he puts it, mental illness should be a transient problem, but medication makes it permanent.

If a drink or two helps others get through the day, then of course that is their decision too. It just would not work for me – in fact as the child of an alcoholic I avoid alcohol as much as possible – I have seen the consequences of addition to it and they are not pleasant. (Incidentally, the mother of a friend of mine, who had a breakdown in the seventies, was advised by her GP to chuck away all the pills that she had been prescribed in the hospital, and have a good glug of whisky instead. She eventually became an alcoholic, but my friend still sees this as preferable to the alternative, that she would become a walking zombie on psychiatric drugs).

There are many ways to deal with emotional problems, and a lot of them are incredibly effective in strengthening the mind and spirit and allowing a person to get on and cope with life's vicissitudes without a permanent external crutch. In my opinion, this is the course of action that should always be followed when necessary. Mental health can take time to improve, and tranquilising drugs may be helpful at first – but slowly other techniques can be applied to help people to cope better with the management of their lives. I will outline some of these techniques in the next section.

I believe that patients should be given an informed choice – told how medications can and can't help, and what the possible adverse effects of them may be. In my own case, the medication I took following my second breakdown prevented me from conceiving – although I asked about this and was expressly told that it would not do so. (Interestingly, the medical notes that I recently requested and paid to access while researching this book tell a different story, but I remain quite clear about what happened here).

I am not anti-psychiatry per se. As I have said, I don't believe that diagnoses are given maliciously or that medications are handed out as a punishment – I think the mental health professionals really believe that these are the best (sometimes the only) tools which they have at their disposal. Although I suffered a certain amount of damage at the hands of psychiatrists, most of the ones I have met have been well-motivated. In fact, the same psychiatrist who now insists that I am schizophrenic and that I should be watchful for further psychotic breakdowns, is the mental health professional who I credit with making the greatest contribution towards my recovery. When he talked to me at length during several appointments after my third episode of psychosis, he helped to re-establish my sense of self-worth. When he referred to that episode as ' your third and final breakdown' he flicked a switch in my mind – from that moment I realised the possibility of putting mental illness in my past and I started to be able to move forward with my life.

However, there really should be more openness around the whole subject. Mental health patients should be treated with more respect – professionals should not simply assume that people are not capable of informed consent. Even in the midst of psychosis, I had periods of lucidity, and I know from speaking to others that this was the case for them too. Kindness and compassion should be the watchwords at all times during treatment.

Mental health professionals could start by admitting that they don't have all the answers. Treatment of mental health is, as Patrick Cockburn said in 'Henry's Demons' the book he co-wrote with his son, a hundred years behind the treatment of physical health. That is just the way things are, and if we can acknowledge it, that will enable us to work better with what we do know.

I started this section on 'what would help?' by advising rejection of the diagnosis, and I hope that I have not strayed too far from this subject to persuade you that that is a necessary action. It really is. As I have said, it may be different for those who are diagnosed with bi-polar disorder or other conditions, but anybody who identifies themselves as 'schizophrenic' can only be taking a step down the long road to despair. Look at the problem as one of emotional distress, however, and it begins to seem far more human, much more manageable. Look at this emotional distress as caused by anxiety (as it always is in one form or another) and it begins to seem soluble. Alleviate the anxiety and the patient will improve. I guarantee it.

Once a person realises that they are not living under a life-sentence, that they can and will recover, they will already have taken an important step towards that recovery. I think it should also be made clear to that person that their 'condition' is not hereditary. Possessing a 'schizophrenia' gene does not make one any more likely to go mad, than the so-called 'obesity gene' ensures that a person will become fat. Any one of us, given conditions that are stressful enough, can suffer mental ill health or breakdown, just any human being can eat too much of the wrong sort of food and thus become overweight. Of course, some people may be more susceptible to these conditions than others, but this does not make it their destiny.

The saddest story I have ever heard in recent years was that of a girl who, diagnosed schizophrenic in her twenties, persuaded her doctors to sterilise her because she never wanted to pass the condition on to her children. I know that patients in mental hospitals used to be sterilised as a matter of course, but I would have thought that any sensible medical professional would know better than to carry out such a course of action in this day and age. But then, I was effectively sterilised by medication (and worse, when I asked about it, was told that this was not the case) and I am sure many other men and women have also experienced this treatment. This cannot be right – surely such action is not in accordance with the Hippocratic Oath to, 'Do no harm'.

I will never deny the fact that I was once very mentally unwell. I do not really mind if it is referred to as mental illness or emotional distress, although I prefer the latter term. But I will never again accept that I had, or have, a brain disease – this is not the truth and never has been, and any psychiatric system that continues to spread this myth is mistaken and wrong and – not to put too fine a point on it – rotten to the core. Similarly, there is no justification for forcing people to take medication. That is brutality – not medicine.

I really hope that, in the future, medicine will move towards a more holistic approach to treatment of mental health problems. Diagnosis might be useful for some people – even I was quite willing to believe the counsellor who told me I had social anxiety disorder, because to me it provided an explanation for the way I was, without making me feel any worse about myself than I already did.

The word schizophrenia will leave the language soon enough. It has to – its use is inhumane. It is a bar to recovery. (I don't like the use of the diagnosis of 'personality disorder' either, but that is another subject). In the meantime, I must advise anyone who has received a diagnosis of schizophrenia to reject it, to move above and beyond it. How obvious can it be - recovery is simply not possible as long as you believe that you have a permanent, incurable and hereditary disease of the brain.

Whatever your diagnosis, I would advise that you move forward and beyond the narrow view of 'mental illness' (which is in itself, really not a very nice or uplifting term). Instead, assure yourself that although you have suffered a nervous breakdown, experienced manifestations of emotional distress, you can and you will move on, and be completely well again. Time is a great healer.

Dr Karl Meninger said that calling someone a schizophrenic is no different from calling them a nigger. I agree. We should not be party to the use of such terminology applied to ourselves or to others, for whatever reason.

WHAT WOULD HAVE HELPED?
6. LOOKING OUTSIDE THE MENTAL HEALTH SYSTEM

A mental health system that we could put our trust in would be a great thing. There may be good people working within our current system, but unfortunately there are also many who do not have the best interests of others at heart. And while there is coercion within the system, patients and ex-patients will not be able to trust those people who are treating them. Diagnosis with the label of schizophrenia is also never going to help, it can only ever damage a person.

As far as the mental health system goes, even a brilliant one is limited as to what it can actually do. In September of 2013 I went to a Mental Health Conference at Bournemouth University and during one talk I attended the speaker made the point that although winning the lottery might help the mental health problems of a lot of people – perhaps even cure them - this is not within the remit of the system.

We could, however, provide financial stability to sufferers. We could give people disability benefits and access to services without labelling them with lifelong 'diseases' or putting them under community treatment orders to ensure that they always take their medication. Under the current system, those who care for 'schizophrenics' actually welcome the label because it gives them access to services. The suffering the label imposes is disregarded for this reason. That should change.

The ideal for anyone who has suffered emotional distress

would be to regain normality – that is, to be accepted into society as a functioning member of it. This would mean benefits initially, during the early stages of convalescence, and then ongoing support for individuals to find a suitable home and suitable work and to regain their confidence. All this should be done non-judgementally. In time, and with luck, the individual would become independent and indistinguishable from anyone else.

There are various ways in which the current system could be improved – for example, it would be useful to have nurses who simply talked and listened to patients, without judging them. It would be great if nursing staff could spend more time actually with the patients rather than in the nursing office. (Of course, some hospitals are better than others – the one I stayed in was the antithesis of therapeutic, but I have learned recently through the local press that it has since had a £14 million makeover, so I am sure that the environment there is now more amenable. I would still opt for private mental health treatment though, if I had a choice).

In any case, the system may change, eventually, over time. Meanwhile, if you are working on your recovery, or trying to help someone you care about through theirs, you can't wait for the system to improve. You do have to work within the system while looking outside it for alternatives. If, for example, your aim is to become medication free, mention it to those you work with and keep mentioning it. Ask for help to achieve your aim. If you work to get better and to stay better – to become healthy in body and mind – if you ask to be supervised when you are reducing the drugs and if you are honest about any symptoms that surface while you are going through the process, you should be able to use the system in your favour.

Two years ago I had cognitive behavioural therapy through the National Health Service, which more or less banished my anxiety. This was a revelation - I had already come a long way, but before this treatment I always felt that I was vulnerable to future breakdown. My nerves were always on edge. Once the anxiety was gone, I felt that my susceptibility to breakdown had vanished too. Which is not to say categorically that it will never happen, since no-one can know what the future holds for them. But I do not feel that I am at risk of it any more than any other member of the general public.

However, it was only the third course of CBT, in my early forties, which did the trick – earlier attempts did not have the same effect. I put this partly down to maturity and the different circumstances of my life when I was older, partly down to the experience of my counsellor and the fact that the therapy itself had improved in the twenty-odd years since I first tried it. What I think it proves is that you should always keep going, always keep trying to find a solution to your problems, because, you never know, it may be just around the next corner.

There are many different kinds of help. In my own case, medication was not helpful – partly because it was forced upon me. If I had asked for it and taken it with the attitude that it was going to help me, it might have been a different matter. (Although I doubt this, because on several occasions between my first and second breakdowns I asked for and received medication from various GPs to help with depression or anxiety and none of this stuff proved to be of much use. In my case, I needed to work out the sources of my problems and deal with them myself. Time has proved to be a great healer too).

Medication can, however, be useful for some people. I know quite a few people who are convinced that it keeps them well and that they could not manage without it. I think differently though – in my opinion the drugs (which are basically tranquilisers) stop working after a while when the body becomes accustomed to them. By this time, though, the 'recovered' person's life has settled down to such an extent that they don't need them any longer. However, they are by then physically addicted to the medication (their brains have become dependent on the chemicals) and subsequent withdrawal may lead to breakdown, if not done properly. When people come off the drugs and get ill, they become convinced that this is because they needed the drugs all along. So they are scared to stop taking them again. In fact, it is often because they have stopped their medication too abruptly and without medical supervision.

I feel increasingly awkward about the medication issue. On the one hand, I am really pleased that I am not on psychiatric drugs and that I was not on it during any of my pregnancies. On the other hand, I am aware that other people depend on their drugs, and believe they are necessary. One lady, after reading my first book, decided to stop taking her drugs, got pregnant and then had a severe breakdown after the baby was born. During this time she was separated from her child and suffered terribly as a result. She wrote a review of my book, on the USA Amazon site, saying that after reading it she had been sure that she could stop taking her drugs and have a wonderful life with her husband and child and that as a consequence she had suffered this devastating experience.

It upset me greatly that this woman considered me partly responsible for her breakdown. I don't want to feel responsible for things that might go wrong if other people stop taking their drugs. But I don't believe either that people should be left on harmful drugs for life just because they, or mental health professionals, are frightened of the consequences if they stop. I am not an expert – I only know that I have coped with my life for many years without psychiatric drugs and that therefore this is a possibility. I am not trying to tell others that they can definitely do so, or even that they should try. I am only saying that it is possible.

A friend of mine has a diagnosis of bi-polar disorder. She had her first and only breakdown after her daughter was born. I told her in conversation one day that I had met a chap at the McPin Foundation where I had just been employed as a peer researcher, who maintained that post-puerperal breakdowns happened because of a magnesium deficit (or was it potassium? I forget now). Anyway, she was really interested to know more, so at her insistence I emailed her a link to his website.

When I sent the link, I told my friend that I had not looked at the site myself and so had no opinion about it. However, after she had looked at the site, she fired off an email pointing out the details of her condition to me and telling me why the drugs she took were vital to her. I was mystified and slightly hurt by this, and I felt it was a little unfair. All I can do, and all I have ever done, is to direct people to the information available, or tell them what has worked for me. I am not telling anyone else what they should do. I could not possibly know.

While I was nearing completion of this book my sister, who is a social worker, called me. Her colleague, she said, had just returned to work having had a severe relapse in her depression. She had been trying to alter her drugs to get pregnant, and this had resulted in the relapse. Would I be willing to talk to her?

I wanted to help, I told my sister, but I really did not feel qualified. I can't tell anyone whether or not to take drugs. If after talking to me and discovering that I manage without them they are tempted to do the same, I don't want to be responsible for any consequences. No, my sister said, this woman wants to be pregnant and take the drugs, but different ones. Well, I replied, I am not sure that would be a good thing for the baby, so I can't recommend that either.

The girl just wanted someone to talk to, to tell her everything will be okay, my sister went on. But I was too frightened of the consequences to myself personally to hold out any hope. Things will turn out okay, I am sure, for most people in time. But the courage to make them okay has to come from within the individual. It helps to know that time itself is the greatest healer of all. Also, recovery itself is an individual thing – a person can take medication and still be recovered. All I am just saying – all that I have ever said - is that a person can sometimes recover without the need for medication – not that they should, or must, or that they will, but that they can.

Eventually, I agreed to correspond with my sister's colleague by email. Hopefully in writing I could explain things better. Failing that, I said, there is lots of literature out there, and my own recovery book should be available soon. It was a cop-out, I knew, but I couldn't help it – I just feel very odd these days about trying to help others, in case I get it wrong!

I do get very emotional about the subject of mental illness. When I hear about someone suffering, I feel a great desire to help. I hate to read about young people harming themselves, or committing suicide, because in my experience of emotional distress, and I have had lots of experience, things always get better. Sometimes, you just have to hold on.

CBT was the best therapy I tried, but there are many other activities and therapies that can be helpful to recovery. Anything that helps with the reduction of stress will be beneficial, since stress is at the root of all illnesses, physical and mental. So, better nutrition, sufficient sleep and so on, as outlined above – combined with yoga, meditation, mindfulness, deep breathing strategies and exercise of all sorts, will definitely help in your efforts to return to full health.

I have found the Alexander technique very useful. This is hard to explain, but basically its essence is to do with the use of the body. The Alexander teacher shows how to move in the correct way, so as to put as little strain on the body as possible. If this is done correctly – and it has to be learned carefully, in one-to-one instruction from a qualified practitioner – it can have a very therapeutic effect on both body and mind. I would definitely recommend giving it a try.

I am sure the list of useful therapies is practically endless. I recently came across an online article about something called compassion focussed therapy. This entails three strands. The first is doing activities or making changes that are kind to oneself. The second is trying to see the good in others and oneself instead of dwelling on the negative aspects of life, and the third is regularly speaking out loud to oneself in a warm, kind tone. I had never heard of CFT before, but I am sure it would be beneficial – just reading about it did me good!

Some 'alternative therapies' such as reiki, aromatherapy or reflexology, might be more useful to some people than to others. I think this might be because the effectiveness of the therapy – and this applies to traditional medicine too – often has as much to do with the practitioner of it as with the activity itself. A really kind, caring person who listens as they administer the treatment, whatever it is, and who inspires confidence in the recipient/patient, will have a much better outcome than somebody who is just doing a job, or somebody who has no interest in the person who they are treating.

Some people have a calming and healing presence, and these people should be sought out as companions in life generally, not just for therapy. If you have a friend like this, make the most of them – although of course, you should be careful to listen as well as to talk! It is also possible to call the Samaritans, or helplines run by Rethink Mental Illness or Mind and talk to people on the phone (I made a call to the Samaritans once – the occasion sticks in my mind because I could not get the other person off the end of the phone when I wanted to

141

say goodbye because someone was knocking at my door! I didn't call the Samaritans again, but it often helped to know that they were there if I ever wanted to talk at length). Mind have a befriending service, which must be a godsend for some people.

There are so many things, not even classed as therapy, which are cheaper and less intrusive than medication. Nutrition can play an important part in recovery – the supporters of Dr Abram Hoffer swear by a process called orthomolecular therapy, which includes, as I understand, large doses of vitamin B3. I personally consider many treatments that involve the healing power of touch – for example massage, manicures and the services of a hairdresser, as very therapeutic. If you have the means, treat yourself or the person you love to any therapy that will enhance your, or their, existence without harming them.

WHAT WOULD HAVE HELPED?
7. GETTING MY MIND ON SIDE

I have already emphasised the importance of hope, and
self-belief. You can and you will recover from serious
mental illness (or emotional distress as I prefer to term
it) and understanding and believing this is a vital part of
the process.

First, you need to recognise that you are in charge of
your own mind. There are 'Hearing Voices' groups all
over this country and in the USA – probably worldwide
– that teach people this. Even those who hear voices –
something that I think must be very hard to bear – can
still take charge of them. Nobody has to do what the
voices tell them. Although they may sound very real to
the person who hears them (I have had the voice hearing
experience just twice myself – the voice was my
mother's and I could have sworn that she was standing
next to me whispering in my ear) they are just an
external manifestation of the person's own inner voice.
Which sounds awful to some people, because the voices
can be mean and vicious, but it is just the subconscious,
often re-iterating things that have been said to the person
or that they have heard and internalised when they were
just a child. It is a malfunction of the brain, but it can be
overcome.

The best advice I was ever given in hospital was by a
visiting rabbi. I confided in him how I was feeling,
babbling away at length about my fears and phobias. He
replied simply, telling me that I should, 'Shut that door'.
I took him to mean that I should shut that place in my
mind that let in the disturbance and confusion, and
remain firmly in the present moment, here and now. I

visualised that door shutting, and found myself in a much more peaceful place, and I have used that tool on many occasions since.

At the time of my third and final breakdown I kept a journal in hospital, in which I recorded my daily activities and thoughts. I often found the nurses reading it and I wanted them to – I knew that if they did so they would realise that however uncommunicative I was, however mad or irrational I might seem, my thoughts were clearer and more ordered than anyone could have guessed.

My personal struggle has been learning to trust myself. It took me a long time to come to the conclusion that what I think of myself is far more important than what anyone else thinks of me.

And I have grown to know myself quite well over the years. I am a bit of a hypochondriac – I often have aches and pains – and I have become aware that although my problems seem to manifest physically, they usually emanate from emotional issues. For example, I suffer from irritable bowel syndrome, which is always worse when I am stressed. (Louise Hay's book Heal Your Life, takes this theory to its extreme – in it she lists various physical issues and names their emotional causes). It is all rather a mystery, but it is becoming increasingly apparent to me that the link between physical and mental health is so strongly interwoven that one day it will seem a marvel that anyone ever endeavoured to understand and treat these issues separately.

I also know that I am very susceptible to the placebo

effect – I am quite suggestible. So, if I have not slept for several nights in a row I start to panic a little. That night, I might take a herbal sleeping remedy – and whether or not such remedies contain sedatives, they will work for me, because I believe that they will. I gain a great benefit from homeopathic remedies, although these might not work for many people. I find the link between attitude of mind and illness very interesting indeed. It seems to be an area of healing that has huge potential, if only we could work out exactly what that link is and how to use it.

As time goes on, I have become gradually more confident in my ability to withstand the vicissitudes of life without breaking down. I came through the trauma of my mother's cancer. I also managed to survive my eldest daughter's severe illness, although I hardly slept a wink during the whole week she spent in hospital. Even though I suffered some sort of mild psychosis after the operation on my bunions several years ago, I returned to normal without any psychiatric intervention. And so I have learned that I know my own weaknesses and strengths, I know what I need to do to stay well and for my own sake and for that of my family, I make the right choices for my health and wellbeing. The older I get, hopefully, the more sensible I will become.

WHAT WOULD HAVE HELPED?
8. NOT CARING

This is probably the single most important strategy I can recommend to those who are recovering from mental breakdown. You need to regain your confidence, and to do this you need to stop caring so much about other people's opinions of you. You must develop more effective personal boundaries.

One of my favourite quotes is by Eleanor Roosevelt. She said, 'No-one can make you feel inferior without your consent'. And it's true. It may take a while to implement, for those of us who have always thought others were better, more valid, wholer people (mainly because they don't have a diagnosis of schizophrenia). But it's vitally important.

I think of all my difficulties now as coming from the root cause of social anxiety and I have a personal theory that almost all mental health problems are caused by anxiety of some kind. In my own case, I was psychotic on three occasions and I am not denying that. But there was a reason for those breakdowns – several reasons in fact, and the primary one was anxiety. So, I suppose I am not actually anti-diagnosis, if the diagnosis is a helpful one, as I have found social anxiety to be in my case. (I don't think certain labels, such as schizophrenia or borderline personality disorder, can ever be helpful though. They de-humanise).

I still worry excessively about what other people think of me. I still try too hard to fit in. But I am conscious of these shortcomings. I remind myself that I am just as good as anyone else. I try not to worry. And gradually as I get older I am becoming less self-conscious and this feels incredibly freeing.

Of course, if you didn't care at all about what other people thought or said or did, you would be a psychopath, which would not be good at all. But, if possible, you need to aim to get to the point where you don't worry about these things. Worrying is pointless – it doesn't change anything and it is damaging.

I personally still have to remind myself that although people are entitled to their opinions about me, they are not necessarily right, and I do not have to pay any attention to them. Also, I don't know what anyone else thinks about anything, unless they tell me. And it's not really my business what anybody else thinks of me. Some people know these things automatically – I seem to have always had trouble believing in myself. I am sure that my low self-esteem – my lack of any real sense of my own value - is why I was susceptible to breakdown.

One thing that helps me now is the thought that everyone in life is acting, to some extent. If you feel insecure, nobody actually knows, unless you tell them or show them by your actions. You can learn to cover up these feelings – and if you put on a show of confidence for long enough you will eventually start to believe in it yourself!

WHAT WOULD HAVE HELPED?
9. FOSTERING INDEPENDENCE

I think it is important for a person's recovery that they should become as independent as possible – even from the family that he or she was born into. I realise that this is a contentious subject – and so I would like to make it clear from the outset that what I am referring to is independence of mind, not physical distance.

I have always been very attached to my siblings – overly attached, I realise now. I was always in the position of supplicant – the one who tried to keep in touch, to hold the family together, long after the others had grown up and made lives of their own. Even after I had my own family, I was still very needy of the attention of my siblings. I would phone them all regularly and whenever possible I would invite them over and set up family gatherings. I did this for many years, long after anyone else had stopped bothering. It took me a while to understand – they had grown up now, and it was time for me to grow up too and stop clinging to them. I needed to move on.

This may sound awfully harsh, especially to those people who feel that they have lost their relatives to mental illness and who want desperately to help nurse them back to health. But the best thing for any individual is to regain their independence. I still love my siblings, of course. I have not fallen out with them and I am always happy to see them whenever I have an opportunity to do so.   But I have only healed properly since I took a step back emotionally, and stopped clinging to them and to the past. Without blaming anybody, I can see that the dynamics of my birth family were part of the reason I became ill in the first place.

(Incidentally, I would refer anyone who is interested in this subject to a work by R. D. Laing and A. Esterson, called 'Sanity, Madness and the Family'. It is a fascinating study of how families can impact on a person's mental health).

I really am not advising that anyone should cut themselves off from their birth family – I have not done so and I never would. But anyone who is in full mental health needs to be aware that there is an essence of themselves that is separate from everyone else, even their family. You should be sure to be proud of who you are as an individual.

I do think that everyone needs social support. If this doesn't come from your birth family, and nowadays it doesn't for a lot of people, you have to find it somewhere else. Now that my daughters are growing up they are great company, but I am aware that my role is to support them emotionally, and never the other way round.

So, make friends. I know that this is really hard when you are suffering emotional distress and lacking in confidence, but it does get easier with time and practice. Participate in social activities, even if they are not the sort of thing you would do if you were better. Get out as much as you can, talk to as many people as possible, put out tendrils. You will be surprised where this can lead.

WHAT WOULD HAVE HELPED?
10. A PET

A pet can be invaluable therapy. A pet can make you feel worthwhile and loved and can help you to keep busy and active. Obviously, I only think this is a good idea if you are in a position to look after your pet properly. But if you are, go for it. Your life will become more stable, less chaotic, when you have someone else to care for.

Any pet is good – again, as long as you have the means to house it, feed it and so on. Personally, I love my dogs and consider that humans are so lucky to have dogs – it is a unique relationship, a companion for life. However, if you want to be a dog owner, you will need to know that you are going to be at home pretty much all day, every day, for the duration of your dog's life. Alternatively, you could borrow somebody else's dog for walks and or/companionship. There is a community called 'Borrow My Doggy' that facilitates such arrangements – you can find them online.

AND FINALLY

Karl Jung said, 'A schizophrenic is no longer a schizophrenic when he feels loved by somebody else'.

Start by loving yourself. You are equal with every other human being on the planet. You deserve the best. You are full of potential and you can achieve anything you set out to do. Believe it and start living.